STRANGE DREAMS

a Journal

by Andy J. Miller

CHRONICLE BOOKS

SAN FRANCISCO

ISBN 978-1-4521-2644-9

MANUFACTURED IN CHINA

ILLUSTRATIONS BY ANDY J. MILLER
DESIGN BY ANDY J. MILLER AND NEIL EGAN

CHRONICLE BOOKS PUBLISHES DISTINCTIVE BOOKS AND GIFTS.
FROM AWARD-WINNING CHILDREN'S TITLES, BESTSELLING COOKBOOKS,
AND ECLECTIC POP CULTURE TO ACCLAIMED WORKS OF ART AND
DESIGN, STATIONERY, AND JOURNALS, WE CRAFT PUBLISHING THAT'S
INSTANTLY RECOGNIZABLE FOR ITS SPIRIT AND CREATIVITY. ENJOY
OUR PUBLISHING AND BECOME PART OF OUR COMMUNITY AT
WWW.CHRONICLEBOOKS.COM

10 9 8 7 6 5

CHRONICLE BOOKS LLC
680 SECOND STREET
SAN FRANCISCO, CA 94107
WWW.CHRONICLEBOOKS.COM

INTRODUCTION

ONCE UPON A TIME THERE WAS A MAN WHO WAS WALKING THROUGH THE WOODS... WELL, IT WASN'T THE WOODS... IT JUST LOOKED LIKE THE WOODS... IT WAS ACTUALLY... OUTER SPACE... AND IT WASN'T REALLY JUST A MAN, IT WAS YOUR BEST FRIEND FROM HIGH SCHOOL, BUT HE LOOKED LIKE TOM SELLECK... WITHOUT THE MUSTACHE... AND THE PERM.

DREAMS CAN BE CRAZY.

I HAVE ALWAYS BEEN FASCINATED WITH THEM. PERSONALLY, I HAVE A HISTORY OF DREAMING FANTASTICALLY BIZARRE DREAMS ALMOST EVERY SINGLE NIGHT.

REFLECTING ON WHY I LOVE DREAMS SO MUCH, I CAME TO THIS CONCLUSION:

DREAMS ARE ABSTRACT STORIES WE TELL OURSELVES WHILE WE ARE ASLEEP.

WHILE WE ARE JUST TRYING TO GET A LITTLE SHUT-EYE, OUR CREATIVE SUBCONSCIOUS PENS ABSTRACT POETRY TO OUR CONSCIOUS MINDS.

WHAT A BEAUTIFUL CONCEPT.

WE SPEND AN AVERAGE OF ONE TO TWO HOURS A NIGHT DREAMING. WHETHER YOU REMEMBER YOUR DREAMS OR NOT, YOU ARE DREAMING, AND THAT IS A LARGE PART OF LIFE THAT SHOULD BE APPRECIATED.

I CREATED THIS JOURNAL TO HELP YOU CAPTURE THESE BEAUTIFUL AND MYSTERIOUS SLIPPERY CREATURES BEFORE THEY EVAPORATE. TAKE THE TIME TO RECORD THE WONDERFUL AND CURIOUS DETAILS, AND IF YOU GAIN SOME INSIGHT ALONG THE WAY, MORE POWER TO YOU.

SO GOOD LUCK TO YOU, DREAMER!

MAY YOU DREAM WILDLY AND JOURNAL THOSE STRANGE DREAMS FEVERISHLY.

- Andy J. Miller

STRANGENESS METER

RIDICULOUSLY BORING	MEH	NORMAL	SAAAAY WHAT!?	HUMAN LANGUAGE CANNOT EXPLAIN THIS!

DREAM THEME

- ☐ ANIMALS
- ☐ FIRE
- ☐ LOSING TEETH
- ☐ SUPERNATURAL

- ☐ BEING CHASED
- ☐ FLYING
- ☐ MONEY
- ☐ TRAVEL

- ☐ BUGS
- ☐ FOOD / DRINK
- ☐ NAKED
- ☐ WATER

- ☐ CHILDHOOD
- ☐ HOME
- ☐ OUT-OF-BODY EXPERIENCE
- ☐ WEATHER

☐ OTHER: _____

MAIN CHARACTERS: _____
_____

LOCATION: _____
_____

OVERALL ATMOSPHERE: _____
_____

☐ BLACK-AND-WHITE ☐ IN-COLOR ☐ PREDOMINANT COLOR: _____
☐ IN THE DREAM ☐ WATCHING THE DREAM HAPPEN ☐ LUCID DREAM ☐ RECURRING
ABOUT THE ☐ PAST ☐ PRESENT ☐ FUTURE

HOW I FELT IN MY DREAM: _____
HOW I FEEL NOW: _____
LAST THING I ATE OR DRANK: _____

LAST THING I REMEMBER BEFORE FALLING ASLEEP: _____
_____

MY
STRANGE
DREAM

DREAM TITLE _____ DATE: _____

_____
_____
_____
_____
_____
_____
_____
_____
_____
_____
_____
_____
_____
_____
_____
_____

VISUAL NOTES:

STRANGENESS METER

|————————|————————|————————|————————|
RIDICULOUSLY   MEH   NORMAL   SAAAAY   HUMAN
BORING   WHAT!?   LANGUAGE
                                                                   CANNOT
                                                                   EXPLAIN THIS!

DREAM THEME

☐ ANIMALS   ☐ BEING CHASED   ☐ BUGS   ☐ CHILDHOOD
☐ FIRE   ☐ FLYING   ☐ FOOD / DRINK   ☐ HOME
☐ LOSING TEETH   ☐ MONEY   ☐ NAKED   ☐ OUT-OF-BODY
                                                           EXPERIENCE
☐ SUPERNATURAL   ☐ TRAVEL   ☐ WATER   ☐ WEATHER

☐ OTHER:_____

MAIN CHARACTERS:_____
_____

LOCATION: _____
_____

OVERALL ATMOSPHERE:_____
_____

☐ BLACK-AND-WHITE ☐ IN-COLOR ☐ PREDOMINANT COLOR:_____

☐ IN THE DREAM ☐ WATCHING THE DREAM HAPPEN ☐ LUCID DREAM ☐ RECURRING
                ABOUT THE ☐ PAST ☐ PRESENT ☐ FUTURE

HOW I FELT IN MY DREAM:_____
HOW I FEEL NOW:_____
LAST THING I ATE OR DRANK: _____
_____
LAST THING I REMEMBER BEFORE FALLING ASLEEP:_____
_____

DREAM TITLE _____ DATE: _____

_____
_____
_____
_____
_____
_____
_____
_____
_____
_____
_____
_____
_____
_____
_____
_____
_____
_____

VISUAL NOTES:

STRANGENESS METER

| RIDICULOUSLY BORING | MEH | NORMAL | SAAAAY WHAT!? | HUMAN LANGUAGE CANNOT EXPLAIN THIS! |

. . . .

DREAM THEME

☐ ANIMALS   ☐ BEING CHASED   ☐ BUGS   ☐ CHILDHOOD
☐ FIRE   ☐ FLYING   ☐ FOOD / DRINK   ☐ HOME
☐ LOSING TEETH   ☐ MONEY   ☐ NAKED   ☐ OUT-OF-BODY EXPERIENCE
☐ SUPERNATURAL   ☐ TRAVEL   ☐ WATER   ☐ WEATHER

☐ OTHER: _____

. . . .

MAIN CHARACTERS: _____

_____

LOCATION: _____

_____

OVERALL ATMOSPHERE: _____

_____

☐ BLACK-AND-WHITE   ☐ IN-COLOR   ☐ PREDOMINANT COLOR: _____

☐ IN THE DREAM   ☐ WATCHING THE DREAM HAPPEN   ☐ LUCID DREAM   ☐ RECURRING
ABOUT THE   ☐ PAST   ☐ PRESENT   ☐ FUTURE

HOW I FELT IN MY DREAM: _____
HOW I FEEL NOW: _____
LAST THING I ATE OR DRANK: _____

_____

LAST THING I REMEMBER BEFORE FALLING ASLEEP: _____

_____

MY
STRANGE
DREAM

DREAM TITLE _____ DATE: _____

_____
_____
_____
_____
_____
_____
_____
_____
_____
_____
_____
_____
_____
_____
_____

VISUAL NOTES:

STRANGENESS METER

RIDICULOUSLY BORING	MEH	NORMAL	SAAAAY WHAT!?	HUMAN LANGUAGE CANNOT EXPLAIN THIS!

DREAM THEME

- ☐ ANIMALS
- ☐ FIRE
- ☐ LOSING TEETH
- ☐ SUPERNATURAL

- ☐ BEING CHASED
- ☐ FLYING
- ☐ MONEY
- ☐ TRAVEL

- ☐ BUGS
- ☐ FOOD / DRINK
- ☐ NAKED
- ☐ WATER

- ☐ CHILDHOOD
- ☐ HOME
- ☐ OUT-OF-BODY EXPERIENCE
- ☐ WEATHER

☐ OTHER:_____

MAIN CHARACTERS:_____

_____

LOCATION: _____

_____

OVERALL ATMOSPHERE: _____

_____

☐ BLACK-AND-WHITE ☐ IN-COLOR ☐ PREDOMINANT COLOR:_____

☐ IN THE DREAM ☐ WATCHING THE DREAM HAPPEN ☐ LUCID DREAM ☐ RECURRING

ABOUT THE ☐ PAST ☐ PRESENT ☐ FUTURE

HOW I FELT IN MY DREAM:_____
HOW I FEEL NOW:_____

LAST THING I ATE OR DRANK: _____

_____

LAST THING I REMEMBER BEFORE FALLING ASLEEP:_____

_____

MY
STRANGE
DREAM

DREAM TITLE _____ DATE: _____

_____
_____
_____
_____
_____
_____
_____
_____
_____
_____
_____
_____
_____
_____
_____
_____

VISUAL NOTES:

STRANGENESS METER

RIDICULOUSLY | MEH | NORMAL | SAAAAY | HUMAN
BORING | | | WHAT!? | LANGUAGE
| | | | CANNOT
| | | | EXPLAIN THIS!

DREAM THEME

☐ ANIMALS   ☐ BEING CHASED   ☐ BUGS   ☐ CHILDHOOD

☐ FIRE   ☐ FLYING   ☐ FOOD / DRINK   ☐ HOME

☐ LOSING TEETH   ☐ MONEY   ☐ NAKED   ☐ OUT-OF-BODY EXPERIENCE

☐ SUPERNATURAL   ☐ TRAVEL   ☐ WATER   ☐ WEATHER

☐ OTHER:_____

MAIN CHARACTERS:_____

_____

LOCATION: _____

_____

OVERALL ATMOSPHERE:_____

_____

☐ BLACK-AND-WHITE   ☐ IN-COLOR   ☐ PREDOMINANT COLOR:_____

☐ IN THE DREAM   ☐ WATCHING THE DREAM HAPPEN   ☐ LUCID DREAM   ☐ RECURRING

ABOUT THE   ☐ PAST   ☐ PRESENT   ☐ FUTURE

HOW I FELT IN MY DREAM:_____

HOW I FEEL NOW: _____

LAST THING I ATE OR DRANK:_____

_____

LAST THING I REMEMBER BEFORE FALLING ASLEEP:_____

_____

MY
STRANGE
DREAM

DREAM TITLE _____ DATE: _____

_____
_____
_____
_____
_____
_____
_____
_____
_____
_____
_____
_____
_____
_____
_____
_____

VISUAL NOTES:

STRANGENESS METER

RIDICULOUSLY BORING	MEH	NORMAL	SAAAAY WHAT!?	HUMAN LANGUAGE CANNOT EXPLAIN THIS!

DREAM THEME

☐ ANIMALS   ☐ BEING CHASED   ☐ BUGS   ☐ CHILDHOOD

☐ FIRE   ☐ FLYING   ☐ FOOD / DRINK   ☐ HOME

☐ LOSING TEETH   ☐ MONEY   ☐ NAKED   ☐ OUT-OF-BODY EXPERIENCE

☐ SUPERNATURAL ☐ TRAVEL   ☐ WATER   ☐ WEATHER

☐ OTHER:_____

MAIN CHARACTERS:_____
_____

LOCATION: _____
_____

OVERALL ATMOSPHERE:_____
_____

☐ BLACK-AND-WHITE ☐ IN-COLOR ☐ PREDOMINANT COLOR:_____

☐ IN THE DREAM ☐ WATCHING THE DREAM HAPPEN ☐ LUCID DREAM ☐ RECURRING

ABOUT THE ☐ PAST ☐ PRESENT ☐ FUTURE

HOW I FELT IN MY DREAM:_____
HOW I FEEL NOW:_____
LAST THING I ATE OR DRANK:_____
_____
LAST THING I REMEMBER BEFORE FALLING ASLEEP:_____
_____

MY
STRANGE
DREAM

DREAM TITLE _____ DATE: _____

_____

_____

_____

_____

_____

_____

_____

_____

_____

_____

_____

_____

_____

_____

VISUAL NOTES:

STRANGENESS METER

RIDICULOUSLY BORING	MEH	NORMAL	SAAAAY WHAT!?	HUMAN LANGUAGE CANNOT EXPLAIN THIS!

DREAM THEME

- ☐ ANIMALS
- ☐ FIRE
- ☐ LOSING TEETH
- ☐ SUPERNATURAL

- ☐ BEING CHASED
- ☐ FLYING
- ☐ MONEY
- ☐ TRAVEL

- ☐ BUGS
- ☐ FOOD / DRINK
- ☐ NAKED
- ☐ WATER

- ☐ CHILDHOOD
- ☐ HOME
- ☐ OUT-OF-BODY EXPERIENCE
- ☐ WEATHER

☐ OTHER:_____

MAIN CHARACTERS:_____

_____

LOCATION: _____

_____

OVERALL ATMOSPHERE:_____

_____

☐ BLACK-AND-WHITE ☐ IN-COLOR ☐ PREDOMINANT COLOR:_____

☐ IN THE DREAM ☐ WATCHING THE DREAM HAPPEN ☐ LUCID DREAM ☐ RECURRING

ABOUT THE ☐ PAST ☐ PRESENT ☐ FUTURE

HOW I FELT IN MY DREAM:_____

HOW I FEEL NOW:_____

LAST THING I ATE OR DRANK:_____

_____

LAST THING I REMEMBER BEFORE FALLING ASLEEP:_____

_____

MY STRANGE DREAM

DREAM TITLE _____ DATE: _____

_____
_____
_____
_____
_____
_____
_____
_____
_____
_____
_____
_____
_____
_____
_____
_____
_____
_____

VISUAL NOTES:

STRANGENESS METER

RIDICULOUSLY BORING | MEH | NORMAL | SAAAAY WHAT!? | HUMAN LANGUAGE CANNOT EXPLAIN THIS!

DREAM THEME

☐ ANIMALS   ☐ BEING CHASED   ☐ BUGS   ☐ CHILDHOOD

☐ FIRE   ☐ FLYING   ☐ FOOD / DRINK   ☐ HOME

☐ LOSING TEETH   ☐ MONEY   ☐ NAKED   ☐ OUT-OF-BODY EXPERIENCE

☐ SUPERNATURAL   ☐ TRAVEL   ☐ WATER   ☐ WEATHER

☐ OTHER: _____

MAIN CHARACTERS: _____

LOCATION: _____

OVERALL ATMOSPHERE: _____

☐ BLACK-AND-WHITE   ☐ IN-COLOR   ☐ PREDOMINANT COLOR: _____

☐ IN THE DREAM   ☐ WATCHING THE DREAM HAPPEN   ☐ LUCID DREAM   ☐ RECURRING

ABOUT THE   ☐ PAST   ☐ PRESENT   ☐ FUTURE

HOW I FELT IN MY DREAM: _____

HOW I FEEL NOW: _____

LAST THING I ATE OR DRANK: _____

LAST THING I REMEMBER BEFORE FALLING ASLEEP: _____

DREAM TITLE _____ DATE: _____

_____
_____
_____
_____
_____
_____
_____
_____
_____
_____
_____
_____
_____
_____
_____
_____

VISUAL NOTES:

STRANGENESS METER

RIDICULOUSLY BORING	MEH	NORMAL	SAAAAY WHAT!?	HUMAN LANGUAGE CANNOT EXPLAIN THIS!

DREAM THEME

☐ ANIMALS ☐ BEING CHASED ☐ BUGS ☐ CHILDHOOD
☐ FIRE ☐ FLYING ☐ FOOD / DRINK ☐ HOME
☐ LOSING TEETH ☐ MONEY ☐ NAKED ☐ OUT-OF-BODY EXPERIENCE
☐ SUPERNATURAL ☐ TRAVEL ☐ WATER ☐ WEATHER

☐ OTHER: _____

MAIN CHARACTERS: _____

_____

LOCATION: _____

_____

OVERALL ATMOSPHERE: _____

_____

☐ BLACK-AND-WHITE ☐ IN-COLOR ☐ PREDOMINANT COLOR: _____

☐ IN THE DREAM ☐ WATCHING THE DREAM HAPPEN ☐ LUCID DREAM ☐ RECURRING

ABOUT THE ☐ PAST ☐ PRESENT ☐ FUTURE

HOW I FELT IN MY DREAM: _____
HOW I FEEL NOW: _____
LAST THING I ATE OR DRANK: _____

_____

LAST THING I REMEMBER BEFORE FALLING ASLEEP: _____

_____

MY
STRANGE
DREAM

DREAM TITLE _____ DATE: _____

_____
_____
_____
_____
_____
_____
_____
_____
_____
_____
_____
_____
_____
_____
_____
_____
_____
_____

VISUAL NOTES:

STRANGENESS METER

RIDICULOUSLY BORING	MEH	NORMAL	SAAAAY WHAT!?	HUMAN LANGUAGE CANNOT EXPLAIN THIS!

DREAM THEME

☐ ANIMALS   ☐ BEING CHASED   ☐ BUGS   ☐ CHILDHOOD

☐ FIRE   ☐ FLYING   ☐ FOOD / DRINK   ☐ HOME

☐ LOSING TEETH   ☐ MONEY   ☐ NAKED   ☐ OUT-OF-BODY EXPERIENCE

☐ SUPERNATURAL   ☐ TRAVEL   ☐ WATER   ☐ WEATHER

☐ OTHER: _____

MAIN CHARACTERS: _____
_____

LOCATION: _____
_____

OVERALL ATMOSPHERE: _____
_____

☐ BLACK-AND-WHITE   ☐ IN-COLOR   ☐ PREDOMINANT COLOR: _____

☐ IN THE DREAM   ☐ WATCHING THE DREAM HAPPEN   ☐ LUCID DREAM   ☐ RECURRING

ABOUT THE   ☐ PAST   ☐ PRESENT   ☐ FUTURE

HOW I FELT IN MY DREAM: _____

HOW I FEEL NOW: _____

LAST THING I ATE OR DRANK: _____
_____

LAST THING I REMEMBER BEFORE FALLING ASLEEP: _____
_____

MY
STRANGE
DREAM

DREAM TITLE _____ DATE: _____

_____
_____
_____
_____
_____
_____
_____
_____
_____
_____
_____
_____
_____
_____

VISUAL NOTES:

STRANGENESS METER

RIDICULOUSLY BORING	MEH	NORMAL	SAAAAY WHAT!?	HUMAN LANGUAGE CANNOT EXPLAIN THIS!

DREAM THEME

☐ ANIMALS   ☐ BEING CHASED   ☐ BUGS   ☐ CHILDHOOD

☐ FIRE   ☐ FLYING   ☐ FOOD / DRINK   ☐ HOME

☐ LOSING TEETH   ☐ MONEY   ☐ NAKED   ☐ OUT-OF-BODY EXPERIENCE

☐ SUPERNATURAL   ☐ TRAVEL   ☐ WATER   ☐ WEATHER

☐ OTHER: _____

MAIN CHARACTERS: _____
_____

LOCATION: _____
_____

OVERALL ATMOSPHERE: _____
_____

☐ BLACK-AND-WHITE   ☐ IN-COLOR   ☐ PREDOMINANT COLOR: _____

☐ IN THE DREAM   ☐ WATCHING THE DREAM HAPPEN   ☐ LUCID DREAM   ☐ RECURRING

ABOUT THE   ☐ PAST   ☐ PRESENT   ☐ FUTURE

HOW I FELT IN MY DREAM: _____

HOW I FEEL NOW: _____

LAST THING I ATE OR DRANK: _____

LAST THING I REMEMBER BEFORE FALLING ASLEEP: _____
_____

MY
STRANGE
DREAM

DREAM TITLE _____ DATE: _____

_____
_____
_____
_____
_____
_____
_____
_____
_____
_____
_____
_____
_____
_____
_____

VISUAL NOTES:

STRANGENESS METER

RIDICULOUSLY BORING | MEH | NORMAL | SAAAAY WHAT!? | HUMAN LANGUAGE CANNOT EXPLAIN THIS!

DREAM THEME

☐ ANIMALS   ☐ BEING CHASED   ☐ BUGS   ☐ CHILDHOOD
☐ FIRE   ☐ FLYING   ☐ FOOD / DRINK ☐ HOME
☐ LOSING TEETH ☐ MONEY   ☐ NAKED   ☐ OUT-OF-BODY EXPERIENCE
☐ SUPERNATURAL ☐ TRAVEL   ☐ WATER   ☐ WEATHER

☐ OTHER: _____

MAIN CHARACTERS: _____

_____

LOCATION: _____

_____

OVERALL ATMOSPHERE: _____

_____

☐ BLACK-AND-WHITE ☐ IN-COLOR ☐ PREDOMINANT COLOR: _____

☐ IN THE DREAM ☐ WATCHING THE DREAM HAPPEN ☐ LUCID DREAM ☐ RECURRING

ABOUT THE ☐ PAST ☐ PRESENT ☐ FUTURE

HOW I FELT IN MY DREAM: _____

HOW I FEEL NOW: _____

LAST THING I ATE OR DRANK: _____

_____

LAST THING I REMEMBER BEFORE FALLING ASLEEP: _____

_____

MY
STRANGE
DREAM

DREAM TITLE _____ DATE: _____

_____
_____
_____
_____
_____
_____
_____
_____
_____
_____
_____
_____
_____
_____

VISUAL NOTES:

STRANGENESS METER

RIDICULOUSLY BORING	MEH	NORMAL	SAAAAY WHAT!?	HUMAN LANGUAGE CAN NOT EXPLAIN THIS!

DREAM THEME

☐ ANIMALS ☐ BEING CHASED ☐ BUGS ☐ CHILDHOOD
☐ FIRE ☐ FLYING ☐ FOOD / DRINK ☐ HOME
☐ LOSING TEETH ☐ MONEY ☐ NAKED ☐ OUT-OF-BODY EXPERIENCE
☐ SUPERNATURAL ☐ TRAVEL ☐ WATER ☐ WEATHER
☐ OTHER: _____

MAIN CHARACTERS: _____
_____

LOCATION: _____
_____

OVERALL ATMOSPHERE: _____
_____

☐ BLACK-AND-WHITE ☐ IN-COLOR ☐ PREDOMINANT COLOR: _____
☐ IN THE DREAM ☐ WATCHING THE DREAM HAPPEN ☐ LUCID DREAM ☐ RECURRING
ABOUT THE ☐ PAST ☐ PRESENT ☐ FUTURE

HOW I FELT IN MY DREAM: _____
HOW I FEEL NOW: _____
LAST THING I ATE OR DRANK: _____
_____

LAST THING I REMEMBER BEFORE FALLING ASLEEP: _____
_____

MY
STRANGE
DREAM

DREAM TITLE _____ DATE: _____

_____
_____
_____
_____
_____
_____
_____
_____
_____
_____
_____
_____
_____
_____
_____

VISUAL NOTES:

STRANGENESS METER

RIDICULOUSLY BORING ——|—— MEH ——|—— NORMAL ——|—— SAAAAY WHAT!? ——|—— HUMAN LANGUAGE CANNOT EXPLAIN THIS!

DREAM THEME

☐ ANIMALS   ☐ BEING CHASED   ☐ BUGS   ☐ CHILDHOOD
☐ FIRE   ☐ FLYING   ☐ FOOD / DRINK   ☐ HOME
☐ LOSING TEETH   ☐ MONEY   ☐ NAKED   ☐ OUT-OF-BODY EXPERIENCE
☐ SUPERNATURAL   ☐ TRAVEL   ☐ WATER   ☐ WEATHER

☐ OTHER:_____

MAIN CHARACTERS:_____
_____

LOCATION: _____
_____

OVERALL ATMOSPHERE:_____
_____

☐ BLACK-AND-WHITE   ☐ IN-COLOR   ☐ PREDOMINANT COLOR:_____

☐ IN THE DREAM   ☐ WATCHING THE DREAM HAPPEN   ☐ LUCID DREAM   ☐ RECURRING

ABOUT THE   ☐ PAST ☐ PRESENT ☐ FUTURE

HOW I FELT IN MY DREAM:_____
HOW I FEEL NOW:_____
LAST THING I ATE OR DRANK:_____
_____

LAST THING I REMEMBER BEFORE FALLING ASLEEP:_____
_____

MY
STRANGE
DREAM

DREAM TITLE _____ DATE: _____

_____
_____
_____
_____
_____
_____
_____
_____
_____
_____
_____
_____
_____
_____
_____
_____
_____

VISUAL NOTES:

STRANGENESS METER

RIDICULOUSLY BORING — MEH — NORMAL — SAAAAY WHAT!? — HUMAN LANGUAGE CANNOT EXPLAIN THIS!

DREAM THEME

☐ ANIMALS   ☐ BEING CHASED   ☐ BUGS   ☐ CHILDHOOD

☐ FIRE   ☐ FLYING   ☐ FOOD / DRINK   ☐ HOME

☐ LOSING TEETH   ☐ MONEY   ☐ NAKED   ☐ OUT-OF-BODY EXPERIENCE

☐ SUPERNATURAL   ☐ TRAVEL   ☐ WATER   ☐ WEATHER

☐ OTHER:_____

MAIN CHARACTERS:_____

LOCATION:_____

OVERALL ATMOSPHERE:_____

☐ BLACK-AND-WHITE   ☐ IN-COLOR   ☐ PREDOMINANT COLOR:_____

☐ IN THE DREAM   ☐ WATCHING THE DREAM HAPPEN   ☐ LUCID DREAM   ☐ RECURRING

ABOUT THE   ☐ PAST   ☐ PRESENT   ☐ FUTURE

HOW I FELT IN MY DREAM:_____

HOW I FEEL NOW:_____

LAST THING I ATE OR DRANK:_____

LAST THING I REMEMBER BEFORE FALLING ASLEEP:_____

MY
STRANGE
DREAM

DREAM TITLE _____ DATE: _____

_____
_____
_____
_____
_____
_____
_____
_____
_____
_____
_____
_____
_____
_____
_____
_____

VISUAL NOTES:

STRANGENESS METER

RIDICULOUSLY BORING	MEH	NORMAL	SAAAAY WHAT!?	HUMAN LANGUAGE CANNOT EXPLAIN THIS!

DREAM THEME

☐ ANIMALS   ☐ BEING CHASED   ☐ BUGS   ☐ CHILDHOOD

☐ FIRE   ☐ FLYING   ☐ FOOD / DRINK   ☐ HOME

☐ LOSING TEETH   ☐ MONEY   ☐ NAKED   ☐ OUT-OF-BODY EXPERIENCE

☐ SUPERNATURAL   ☐ TRAVEL   ☐ WATER   ☐ WEATHER

☐ OTHER:_____

MAIN CHARACTERS:_____
_____

LOCATION: _____
_____

OVERALL ATMOSPHERE:_____
_____

☐ BLACK-AND-WHITE ☐ IN-COLOR ☐ PREDOMINANT COLOR:_____

☐ IN THE DREAM ☐ WATCHING THE DREAM HAPPEN ☐ LUCID DREAM ☐ RECURRING

ABOUT THE ☐ PAST ☐ PRESENT ☐ FUTURE

HOW I FELT IN MY DREAM:_____
HOW I FEEL NOW: _____
LAST THING I ATE OR DRANK:_____

LAST THING I REMEMBER BEFORE FALLING ASLEEP:_____
_____

MY
STRANGE
DREAM

DREAM TITLE _____ DATE: _____

_____
_____
_____
_____
_____
_____
_____
_____
_____
_____
_____
_____
_____
_____
_____
_____
_____
_____

VISUAL NOTES:

STRANGENESS METER

RIDICULOUSLY BORING	MEH	NORMAL	SAAAAY WHAT!?	HUMAN LANGUAGE CANNOT EXPLAIN THIS!

DREAM THEME

☐ ANIMALS   ☐ BEING CHASED   ☐ BUGS   ☐ CHILDHOOD

☐ FIRE   ☐ FLYING   ☐ FOOD / DRINK   ☐ HOME

☐ LOSING TEETH   ☐ MONEY   ☐ NAKED   ☐ OUT-OF-BODY EXPERIENCE

☐ SUPERNATURAL   ☐ TRAVEL   ☐ WATER   ☐ WEATHER

☐ OTHER:_____

MAIN CHARACTERS:_____
_____

LOCATION: _____
_____

OVERALL ATMOSPHERE:_____
_____

☐ BLACK-AND-WHITE ☐ IN-COLOR ☐ PREDOMINANT COLOR:_____

☐ IN THE DREAM ☐ WATCHING THE DREAM HAPPEN ☐ LUCID DREAM ☐ RECURRING

ABOUT THE ☐ PAST ☐ PRESENT ☐ FUTURE

HOW I FELT IN MY DREAM:_____

HOW I FEEL NOW:_____

LAST THING I ATE OR DRANK: _____

LAST THING I REMEMBER BEFORE FALLING ASLEEP:_____
_____

MY
STRANGE
DREAM

DREAM TITLE _____ DATE: _____

_____
_____
_____
_____
_____
_____
_____
_____
_____
_____
_____
_____
_____
_____
_____
_____

VISUAL NOTES:

STRANGENESS METER

RIDICULOUSLY BORING	MEH	NORMAL	SAAAAY WHAT!?	HUMAN LANGUAGE CANNOT EXPLAIN THIS!

DREAM THEME

- ☐ ANIMALS
- ☐ FIRE
- ☐ LOSING TEETH
- ☐ SUPERNATURAL

- ☐ BEING CHASED
- ☐ FLYING
- ☐ MONEY
- ☐ TRAVEL

- ☐ BUGS
- ☐ FOOD / DRINK
- ☐ NAKED
- ☐ WATER

- ☐ CHILDHOOD
- ☐ HOME
- ☐ OUT-OF-BODY EXPERIENCE
- ☐ WEATHER

☐ OTHER: _____

MAIN CHARACTERS: _____

LOCATION: _____

OVERALL ATMOSPHERE: _____

☐ BLACK-AND-WHITE ☐ IN-COLOR ☐ PREDOMINANT COLOR: _____

☐ IN THE DREAM ☐ WATCHING THE DREAM HAPPEN ☐ LUCID DREAM ☐ RECURRING

ABOUT THE ☐ PAST ☐ PRESENT ☐ FUTURE

HOW I FELT IN MY DREAM: _____

HOW I FEEL NOW: _____

LAST THING I ATE OR DRANK: _____

LAST THING I REMEMBER BEFORE FALLING ASLEEP: _____

DREAM TITLE _____ DATE: _____

_____
_____
_____
_____
_____
_____
_____
_____
_____
_____
_____
_____
_____
_____

VISUAL NOTES:

STRANGENESS METER

RIDICULOUSLY BORING — MEH — NORMAL — SAAAAY WHAT!? — HUMAN LANGUAGE CANNOT EXPLAIN THIS!

· ·

DREAM THEME

☐ ANIMALS   ☐ BEING CHASED   ☐ BUGS   ☐ CHILDHOOD

☐ FIRE   ☐ FLYING   ☐ FOOD / DRINK   ☐ HOME

☐ LOSING TEETH   ☐ MONEY   ☐ NAKED   ☐ OUT-OF-BODY EXPERIENCE

☐ SUPERNATURAL   ☐ TRAVEL   ☐ WATER   ☐ WEATHER

☐ OTHER:_____

· ·

MAIN CHARACTERS:_____

_____

LOCATION: _____

_____

OVERALL ATMOSPHERE:_____

_____

☐ BLACK-AND-WHITE   ☐ IN-COLOR   ☐ PREDOMINANT COLOR:_____

☐ IN THE DREAM   ☐ WATCHING THE DREAM HAPPEN   ☐ LUCID DREAM   ☐ RECURRING

ABOUT THE   ☐ PAST   ☐ PRESENT   ☐ FUTURE

HOW I FELT IN MY DREAM:_____

HOW I FEEL NOW: _____

LAST THING I ATE OR DRANK:_____

_____

LAST THING I REMEMBER BEFORE FALLING ASLEEP:_____

_____

MY
STRANGE
DREAM

DREAM TITLE _____ DATE: _____

_____
_____
_____
_____
_____
_____
_____
_____
_____
_____
_____
_____
_____
_____
_____

VISUAL NOTES:

STRANGENESS METER

RIDICULOUSLY BORING	MEH	NORMAL	SAAAAY WHAT!?	HUMAN LANGUAGE CANNOT EXPLAIN THIS!

DREAM THEME

☐ ANIMALS   ☐ BEING CHASED   ☐ BUGS   ☐ CHILDHOOD

☐ FIRE   ☐ FLYING   ☐ FOOD / DRINK   ☐ HOME

☐ LOSING TEETH   ☐ MONEY   ☐ NAKED   ☐ OUT-OF-BODY EXPERIENCE

☐ SUPERNATURAL   ☐ TRAVEL   ☐ WATER   ☐ WEATHER

☐ OTHER:_____

MAIN CHARACTERS:_____
_____

LOCATION:_____
_____

OVERALL ATMOSPHERE:_____
_____

☐ BLACK-AND-WHITE   ☐ IN-COLOR   ☐ PREDOMINANT COLOR:_____

☐ IN THE DREAM   ☐ WATCHING THE DREAM HAPPEN   ☐ LUCID DREAM   ☐ RECURRING

ABOUT THE   ☐ PAST   ☐ PRESENT   ☐ FUTURE

HOW I FELT IN MY DREAM:_____

HOW I FEEL NOW:_____

LAST THING I ATE OR DRANK:_____
_____

LAST THING I REMEMBER BEFORE FALLING ASLEEP:_____
_____

MY STRANGE DREAM

DREAM TITLE _____ DATE: _____

_____
_____
_____
_____
_____
_____
_____
_____
_____
_____
_____
_____
_____
_____
_____
_____
_____

VISUAL NOTES:

STRANGENESS METER

RIDICULOUSLY BORING	MEH	NORMAL	SAAAAY WHAT!?	HUMAN LANGUAGE CANNOT EXPLAIN THIS!

DREAM THEME

☐ ANIMALS   ☐ BEING CHASED   ☐ BUGS   ☐ CHILDHOOD

☐ FIRE   ☐ FLYING   ☐ FOOD / DRINK ☐ HOME

☐ LOSING TEETH   ☐ MONEY   ☐ NAKED   ☐ OUT-OF-BODY EXPERIENCE

☐ SUPERNATURAL   ☐ TRAVEL   ☐ WATER   ☐ WEATHER

☐ OTHER: _____

MAIN CHARACTERS: _____
_____

LOCATION: _____
_____

OVERALL ATMOSPHERE: _____
_____

☐ BLACK-AND-WHITE ☐ IN-COLOR ☐ PREDOMINANT COLOR: _____

☐ IN THE DREAM ☐ WATCHING THE DREAM HAPPEN ☐ LUCID DREAM ☐ RECURRING

ABOUT THE ☐ PAST ☐ PRESENT ☐ FUTURE

HOW I FELT IN MY DREAM: _____
HOW I FEEL NOW: _____
LAST THING I ATE OR DRANK: _____

LAST THING I REMEMBER BEFORE FALLING ASLEEP: _____
_____

MY STRANGE DREAM

DREAM TITLE _____ DATE: _____

_____
_____
_____
_____
_____
_____
_____
_____
_____
_____
_____
_____
_____
_____

VISUAL NOTES:

STRANGENESS METER

RIDICULOUSLY BORING	MEH	NORMAL	SAAAAY WHAT!?

HUMAN LANGUAGE CANNOT EXPLAIN THIS!

· ·

DREAM THEME

☐ ANIMALS   ☐ BEING CHASED   ☐ BUGS   ☐ CHILDHOOD

☐ FIRE   ☐ FLYING   ☐ FOOD / DRINK   ☐ HOME

☐ LOSING TEETH ☐ MONEY   ☐ NAKED   ☐ OUT-OF-BODY EXPERIENCE

☐ SUPERNATURAL ☐ TRAVEL   ☐ WATER   ☐ WEATHER

☐ OTHER:_____

· ·

MAIN CHARACTERS:_____

_____

LOCATION: _____

_____

OVERALL ATMOSPHERE: _____

_____

☐ BLACK-AND-WHITE ☐ IN-COLOR ☐ PREDOMINANT COLOR:_____

☐ IN THE DREAM ☐ WATCHING THE DREAM HAPPEN ☐ LUCID DREAM ☐ RECURRING

ABOUT THE ☐ PAST ☐ PRESENT ☐ FUTURE

HOW I FELT IN MY DREAM:_____

HOW I FEEL NOW: _____

LAST THING I ATE OR DRANK:_____

_____

LAST THING I REMEMBER BEFORE FALLING ASLEEP:_____

_____

MY STRANGE DREAM

DREAM TITLE _____ DATE: _____

_____
_____
_____
_____
_____
_____
_____
_____
_____
_____
_____
_____
_____
_____
_____
_____

VISUAL NOTES:

STRANGENESS METER

RIDICULOUSLY BORING	MEH	NORMAL	SAAAAY WHAT!?	HUMAN LANGUAGE CANNOT EXPLAIN THIS!

DREAM THEME

☐ ANIMALS   ☐ BEING CHASED   ☐ BUGS   ☐ CHILDHOOD

☐ FIRE   ☐ FLYING   ☐ FOOD / DRINK   ☐ HOME

☐ LOSING TEETH ☐ MONEY   ☐ NAKED   ☐ OUT-OF-BODY EXPERIENCE

☐ SUPERNATURAL ☐ TRAVEL   ☐ WATER   ☐ WEATHER

☐ OTHER: _____

MAIN CHARACTERS: _____

LOCATION: _____

OVERALL ATMOSPHERE: _____

☐ BLACK-AND-WHITE   ☐ IN-COLOR   ☐ PREDOMINANT COLOR: _____

☐ IN THE DREAM   ☐ WATCHING THE DREAM HAPPEN   ☐ LUCID DREAM   ☐ RECURRING

ABOUT THE   ☐ PAST   ☐ PRESENT   ☐ FUTURE

HOW I FELT IN MY DREAM: _____

HOW I FEEL NOW: _____

LAST THING I ATE OR DRANK: _____

LAST THING I REMEMBER BEFORE FALLING ASLEEP: _____

MY
STRANGE
DREAM

DREAM TITLE _____ DATE: _____

_____
_____
_____
_____
_____
_____
_____
_____
_____
_____
_____
_____
_____
_____
_____
_____
_____

VISUAL NOTES:

STRANGENESS METER

RIDICULOUSLY BORING — MEH — NORMAL — SAAAAY WHAT!? — HUMAN LANGUAGE CANNOT EXPLAIN THIS!

DREAM THEME

☐ ANIMALS   ☐ BEING CHASED   ☐ BUGS   ☐ CHILDHOOD
☐ FIRE   ☐ FLYING   ☐ FOOD / DRINK   ☐ HOME
☐ LOSING TEETH   ☐ MONEY   ☐ NAKED   ☐ OUT-OF-BODY EXPERIENCE
☐ SUPERNATURAL   ☐ TRAVEL   ☐ WATER   ☐ WEATHER

☐ OTHER: _____

MAIN CHARACTERS: _____
_____

LOCATION: _____
_____

OVERALL ATMOSPHERE: _____
_____

☐ BLACK-AND-WHITE ☐ IN-COLOR ☐ PREDOMINANT COLOR: _____

☐ IN THE DREAM ☐ WATCHING THE DREAM HAPPEN ☐ LUCID DREAM ☐ RECURRING
ABOUT THE ☐ PAST ☐ PRESENT ☐ FUTURE

HOW I FELT IN MY DREAM: _____
HOW I FEEL NOW: _____
LAST THING I ATE OR DRANK: _____
_____
LAST THING I REMEMBER BEFORE FALLING ASLEEP: _____
_____

MY STRANGE DREAM

DREAM TITLE _____ DATE: _____

_____
_____
_____
_____
_____
_____
_____
_____
_____
_____
_____
_____
_____
_____
_____

VISUAL NOTES:

STRANGENESS METER

RIDICULOUSLY BORING — MEH — NORMAL — SAAAAY WHAT!? — HUMAN LANGUAGE CANNOT EXPLAIN THIS!

DREAM THEME

- ☐ ANIMALS
- ☐ FIRE
- ☐ LOSING TEETH
- ☐ SUPERNATURAL

- ☐ BEING CHASED
- ☐ FLYING
- ☐ MONEY
- ☐ TRAVEL

- ☐ BUGS
- ☐ FOOD / DRINK
- ☐ NAKED
- ☐ WATER

- ☐ CHILDHOOD
- ☐ HOME
- ☐ OUT-OF-BODY EXPERIENCE
- ☐ WEATHER

☐ OTHER: _____

MAIN CHARACTERS: _____
_____

LOCATION: _____
_____

OVERALL ATMOSPHERE: _____
_____

☐ BLACK-AND-WHITE ☐ IN-COLOR ☐ PREDOMINANT COLOR: _____

☐ IN THE DREAM ☐ WATCHING THE DREAM HAPPEN ☐ LUCID DREAM ☐ RECURRING

ABOUT THE ☐ PAST ☐ PRESENT ☐ FUTURE

HOW I FELT IN MY DREAM: _____
HOW I FEEL NOW: _____
LAST THING I ATE OR DRANK: _____
_____
LAST THING I REMEMBER BEFORE FALLING ASLEEP: _____
_____

MY
STRANGE
DREAM

DREAM TITLE _____ DATE: _____

_____
_____
_____
_____
_____
_____
_____
_____
_____
_____
_____
_____
_____
_____
_____

VISUAL NOTES:

STRANGENESS METER

RIDICULOUSLY BORING   MEH   NORMAL   SAAAAY WHAT!?   HUMAN LANGUAGE CANNOT EXPLAIN THIS!

DREAM THEME

- ☐ ANIMALS
- ☐ FIRE
- ☐ LOSING TEETH
- ☐ SUPERNATURAL

- ☐ BEING CHASED
- ☐ FLYING
- ☐ MONEY
- ☐ TRAVEL

- ☐ BUGS
- ☐ FOOD / DRINK
- ☐ NAKED
- ☐ WATER

- ☐ CHILDHOOD
- ☐ HOME
- ☐ OUT-OF-BODY EXPERIENCE
- ☐ WEATHER

☐ OTHER: _____

MAIN CHARACTERS: _____
_____

LOCATION: _____
_____

OVERALL ATMOSPHERE: _____
_____

☐ BLACK-AND-WHITE   ☐ IN-COLOR   ☐ PREDOMINANT COLOR: _____

☐ IN THE DREAM   ☐ WATCHING THE DREAM HAPPEN   ☐ LUCID DREAM   ☐ RECURRING

ABOUT THE   ☐ PAST   ☐ PRESENT   ☐ FUTURE

HOW I FELT IN MY DREAM: _____
HOW I FEEL NOW: _____
LAST THING I ATE OR DRANK: _____
_____

LAST THING I REMEMBER BEFORE FALLING ASLEEP: _____
_____

MY
STRANGE
DREAM

DREAM TITLE _____ DATE: _____

_____
_____
_____
_____
_____
_____
_____
_____
_____
_____
_____
_____
_____
_____
_____

VISUAL NOTES:

STRANGENESS METER

RIDICULOUSLY BORING	MEH	NORMAL	SAAAAY WHAT!?	HUMAN LANGUAGE CANNOT EXPLAIN THIS!

DREAM THEME

☐ ANIMALS   ☐ BEING CHASED   ☐ BUGS   ☐ CHILDHOOD

☐ FIRE   ☐ FLYING   ☐ FOOD / DRINK   ☐ HOME

☐ LOSING TEETH   ☐ MONEY   ☐ NAKED   ☐ OUT-OF-BODY EXPERIENCE

☐ SUPERNATURAL   ☐ TRAVEL   ☐ WATER   ☐ WEATHER

☐ OTHER: _____

MAIN CHARACTERS: _____

_____

LOCATION: _____

_____

OVERALL ATMOSPHERE: _____

_____

☐ BLACK-AND-WHITE   ☐ IN-COLOR   ☐ PREDOMINANT COLOR: _____

☐ IN THE DREAM   ☐ WATCHING THE DREAM HAPPEN   ☐ LUCID DREAM   ☐ RECURRING

ABOUT THE   ☐ PAST   ☐ PRESENT   ☐ FUTURE

HOW I FELT IN MY DREAM: _____

HOW I FEEL NOW: _____

LAST THING I ATE OR DRANK: _____

LAST THING I REMEMBER BEFORE FALLING ASLEEP: _____

_____

MY
STRANGE
DREAM

DREAM TITLE _____ DATE: _____

_____
_____
_____
_____
_____
_____
_____
_____
_____
_____
_____
_____
_____
_____

VISUAL NOTES:

STRANGENESS METER

RIDICULOUSLY BORING	MEH	NORMAL	SAAAAY WHAT!?	HUMAN LANGUAGE CANNOT EXPLAIN THIS!

DREAM THEME

□ ANIMALS   □ BEING CHASED   □ BUGS   □ CHILDHOOD

□ FIRE   □ FLYING   □ FOOD / DRINK   □ HOME

□ LOSING TEETH   □ MONEY   □ NAKED   □ OUT-OF-BODY EXPERIENCE

□ SUPERNATURAL   □ TRAVEL   □ WATER   □ WEATHER

□ OTHER:_____

MAIN CHARACTERS:_____

_____

LOCATION: _____

_____

OVERALL ATMOSPHERE:_____

_____

□ BLACK-AND-WHITE   □ IN-COLOR   □ PREDOMINANT COLOR:_____

□ IN THE DREAM   □ WATCHING THE DREAM HAPPEN   □ LUCID DREAM   □ RECURRING

ABOUT THE   □ PAST   □ PRESENT   □ FUTURE

HOW I FELT IN MY DREAM:_____

HOW I FEEL NOW: _____

LAST THING I ATE OR DRANK: _____

_____

LAST THING I REMEMBER BEFORE FALLING ASLEEP:_____

_____

MY
STRANGE
DREAM

DREAM TITLE _____ DATE: _____

_____
_____
_____
_____
_____
_____
_____
_____
_____
_____
_____
_____
_____
_____
_____
_____

VISUAL NOTES:

STRANGENESS METER

RIDICULOUSLY BORING	MEH	NORMAL	SAAAAY WHAT!?	HUMAN LANGUAGE CANNOT EXPLAIN THIS!

DREAM THEME

☐ ANIMALS   ☐ BEING CHASED   ☐ BUGS   ☐ CHILDHOOD

☐ FIRE   ☐ FLYING   ☐ FOOD / DRINK ☐ HOME

☐ LOSING TEETH   ☐ MONEY   ☐ NAKED   ☐ OUT-OF-BODY EXPERIENCE

☐ SUPERNATURAL   ☐ TRAVEL   ☐ WATER   ☐ WEATHER

☐ OTHER: _____

MAIN CHARACTERS: _____

LOCATION: _____

OVERALL ATMOSPHERE: _____

☐ BLACK-AND-WHITE ☐ IN-COLOR ☐ PREDOMINANT COLOR: _____

☐ IN THE DREAM ☐ WATCHING THE DREAM HAPPEN ☐ LUCID DREAM ☐ RECURRING

ABOUT THE ☐ PAST ☐ PRESENT ☐ FUTURE

HOW I FELT IN MY DREAM: _____
HOW I FEEL NOW: _____

LAST THING I ATE OR DRANK: _____

LAST THING I REMEMBER BEFORE FALLING ASLEEP: _____

MY
STRANGE
DREAM

DREAM TITLE _____ DATE: _____

_____
_____
_____
_____
_____
_____
_____
_____
_____
_____
_____
_____
_____
_____
_____
_____
_____

VISUAL NOTES:

STRANGENESS METER

RIDICULOUSLY
BORING — MEH — NORMAL — SAAAAY
WHAT!? — HUMAN
LANGUAGE
CANNOT
EXPLAIN THIS!

DREAM THEME

☐ ANIMALS   ☐ BEING CHASED   ☐ BUGS   ☐ CHILDHOOD

☐ FIRE   ☐ FLYING   ☐ FOOD / DRINK ☐ HOME

☐ LOSING TEETH ☐ MONEY   ☐ NAKED   ☐ OUT-OF-BODY
                                                   EXPERIENCE

☐ SUPERNATURAL ☐ TRAVEL   ☐ WATER   ☐ WEATHER

☐ OTHER:_____

MAIN CHARACTERS:_____
_____

LOCATION: _____
_____

OVERALL ATMOSPHERE:_____
_____

☐ BLACK-AND-WHITE   ☐ IN-COLOR   ☐ PREDOMINANT COLOR:_____

☐ IN THE DREAM   ☐ WATCHING THE DREAM HAPPEN   ☐ LUCID DREAM   ☐ RECURRING
            ABOUT THE   ☐ PAST   ☐ PRESENT   ☐ FUTURE

HOW I FELT IN MY DREAM:_____
HOW I FEEL NOW:_____
LAST THING I ATE OR DRANK:_____
_____
LAST THING I REMEMBER BEFORE FALLING ASLEEP:_____
_____

MY
STRANGE
DREAM

DREAM TITLE _____ DATE: _____

_____

_____

_____

_____

_____

_____

_____

_____

_____

_____

_____

_____

_____

_____

_____

_____

VISUAL NOTES:

STRANGENESS METER

RIDICULOUSLY BORING — MEH — NORMAL — SAAAAY WHAT!? — HUMAN LANGUAGE CANNOT EXPLAIN THIS!

DREAM THEME

☐ ANIMALS   ☐ BEING CHASED   ☐ BUGS   ☐ CHILDHOOD

☐ FIRE   ☐ FLYING   ☐ FOOD / DRINK   ☐ HOME

☐ LOSING TEETH   ☐ MONEY   ☐ NAKED   ☐ OUT-OF-BODY EXPERIENCE

☐ SUPERNATURAL   ☐ TRAVEL   ☐ WATER   ☐ WEATHER

☐ OTHER: _____

MAIN CHARACTERS: _____

_____

LOCATION: _____

_____

OVERALL ATMOSPHERE: _____

_____

☐ BLACK-AND-WHITE   ☐ IN-COLOR   ☐ PREDOMINANT COLOR: _____

☐ IN THE DREAM   ☐ WATCHING THE DREAM HAPPEN   ☐ LUCID DREAM   ☐ RECURRING

ABOUT THE   ☐ PAST   ☐ PRESENT   ☐ FUTURE

HOW I FELT IN MY DREAM: _____

HOW I FEEL NOW: _____

LAST THING I ATE OR DRANK: _____

_____

LAST THING I REMEMBER BEFORE FALLING ASLEEP: _____

_____

DREAM TITLE _____ DATE: _____

VISUAL NOTES:

STRANGENESS METER

RIDICULOUSLY BORING — MEH — NORMAL — SAAAAY WHAT!? — HUMAN LANGUAGE CANNOT EXPLAIN THIS!

DREAM THEME

☐ ANIMALS   ☐ BEING CHASED   ☐ BUGS   ☐ CHILDHOOD
☐ FIRE   ☐ FLYING   ☐ FOOD / DRINK ☐ HOME
☐ LOSING TEETH ☐ MONEY   ☐ NAKED   ☐ OUT-OF-BODY EXPERIENCE
☐ SUPERNATURAL ☐ TRAVEL   ☐ WATER   ☐ WEATHER

☐ OTHER:_____

MAIN CHARACTERS:_____
_____

LOCATION: _____
_____

OVERALL ATMOSPHERE: _____
_____

☐ BLACK-AND-WHITE ☐ IN-COLOR ☐ PREDOMINANT COLOR:_____

☐ IN THE DREAM ☐ WATCHING THE DREAM HAPPEN ☐ LUCID DREAM ☐ RECURRING
ABOUT THE ☐ PAST ☐ PRESENT ☐ FUTURE

HOW I FELT IN MY DREAM:_____
HOW I FEEL NOW:_____
LAST THING I ATE OR DRANK:_____
_____

LAST THING I REMEMBER BEFORE FALLING ASLEEP:_____
_____

MY
STRANGE
DREAM

DREAM TITLE _____ DATE: _____

_____
_____
_____
_____
_____
_____
_____
_____
_____
_____
_____
_____
_____
_____
_____
_____

VISUAL NOTES:

STRANGENESS METER

RIDICULOUSLY BORING	MEH	NORMAL	SAAAAY WHAT!?	HUMAN LANGUAGE CANNOT EXPLAIN THIS!

. . . .

DREAM THEME

☐ ANIMALS   ☐ BEING CHASED   ☐ BUGS   ☐ CHILDHOOD

☐ FIRE   ☐ FLYING   ☐ FOOD / DRINK   ☐ HOME

☐ LOSING TEETH   ☐ MONEY   ☐ NAKED   ☐ OUT-OF-BODY EXPERIENCE

☐ SUPERNATURAL   ☐ TRAVEL   ☐ WATER   ☐ WEATHER

☐ OTHER: _____

. . . .

MAIN CHARACTERS: _____

_____

LOCATION: _____

_____

OVERALL ATMOSPHERE: _____

_____

☐ BLACK-AND-WHITE   ☐ IN-COLOR   ☐ PREDOMINANT COLOR: _____

☐ IN THE DREAM   ☐ WATCHING THE DREAM HAPPEN   ☐ LUCID DREAM   ☐ RECURRING

ABOUT THE   ☐ PAST   ☐ PRESENT   ☐ FUTURE

HOW I FELT IN MY DREAM: _____

HOW I FEEL NOW: _____

LAST THING I ATE OR DRANK: _____

_____

LAST THING I REMEMBER BEFORE FALLING ASLEEP: _____

_____

MY
STRANGE
DREAM

DREAM TITLE _____ DATE: _____

_____
_____
_____
_____
_____
_____
_____
_____
_____
_____
_____
_____
_____
_____
_____
_____

VISUAL NOTES:

STRANGENESS METER

RIDICULOUSLY BORING	MEH	NORMAL	SAAAAY WHAT!?	HUMAN LANGUAGE CANNOT EXPLAIN THIS!

. . . .

DREAM THEME

☐ ANIMALS   ☐ BEING CHASED   ☐ BUGS   ☐ CHILDHOOD

☐ FIRE   ☐ FLYING   ☐ FOOD / DRINK   ☐ HOME

☐ LOSING TEETH   ☐ MONEY   ☐ NAKED   ☐ OUT-OF-BODY EXPERIENCE

☐ SUPERNATURAL   ☐ TRAVEL   ☐ WATER   ☐ WEATHER

☐ OTHER:_____

. . . .

MAIN CHARACTERS:_____

_____

LOCATION: _____

_____

OVERALL ATMOSPHERE:_____

_____

☐ BLACK-AND-WHITE ☐ IN-COLOR ☐ PREDOMINANT COLOR:_____

☐ IN THE DREAM ☐ WATCHING THE DREAM HAPPEN ☐ LUCID DREAM ☐ RECURRING

ABOUT THE ☐ PAST ☐ PRESENT ☐ FUTURE

HOW I FELT IN MY DREAM:_____

HOW I FEEL NOW:_____

LAST THING I ATE OR DRANK:_____

_____

LAST THING I REMEMBER BEFORE FALLING ASLEEP:_____

_____

MY
STRANGE
DREAM

DREAM TITLE _____ DATE: _____

_____
_____
_____
_____
_____
_____
_____
_____
_____
_____
_____
_____
_____
_____
_____

VISUAL NOTES:

STRANGENESS METER

|——————————|——————————|——————————|——————————|
RIDICULOUSLY   MEH   NORMAL   SAAAAY   HUMAN
BORING   WHAT!?   LANGUAGE
                                                                   CANNOT
                                                                   EXPLAIN THIS!

DREAM THEME

☐ ANIMALS   ☐ BEING CHASED   ☐ BUGS   ☐ CHILDHOOD
☐ FIRE   ☐ FLYING   ☐ FOOD / DRINK   ☐ HOME
☐ LOSING TEETH   ☐ MONEY   ☐ NAKED   ☐ OUT-OF-BODY
                                                          EXPERIENCE
☐ SUPERNATURAL   ☐ TRAVEL   ☐ WATER   ☐ WEATHER

☐ OTHER: _____

MAIN CHARACTERS: _____
_____

LOCATION: _____
_____

OVERALL ATMOSPHERE: _____
_____

☐ BLACK-AND-WHITE   ☐ IN-COLOR   ☐ PREDOMINANT COLOR: _____

☐ IN THE DREAM   ☐ WATCHING THE DREAM HAPPEN   ☐ LUCID DREAM   ☐ RECURRING

ABOUT THE   ☐ PAST   ☐ PRESENT   ☐ FUTURE

HOW I FELT IN MY DREAM: _____
HOW I FEEL NOW: _____
LAST THING I ATE OR DRANK: _____
_____

LAST THING I REMEMBER BEFORE FALLING ASLEEP: _____
_____

MY STRANGE DREAM

DREAM TITLE _____ DATE: _____

_____
_____
_____
_____
_____
_____
_____
_____
_____
_____
_____
_____
_____
_____
_____
_____

VISUAL NOTES:

STRANGENESS METER

RIDICULOUSLY BORING	MEH	NORMAL	SAAAAY WHAT!?	HUMAN LANGUAGE CANNOT EXPLAIN THIS!

DREAM THEME

☐ ANIMALS   ☐ BEING CHASED   ☐ BUGS   ☐ CHILDHOOD

☐ FIRE   ☐ FLYING   ☐ FOOD / DRINK   ☐ HOME

☐ LOSING TEETH   ☐ MONEY   ☐ NAKED   ☐ OUT-OF-BODY EXPERIENCE

☐ SUPERNATURAL   ☐ TRAVEL   ☐ WATER   ☐ WEATHER

☐ OTHER:_____

MAIN CHARACTERS:_____
_____

LOCATION: _____
_____

OVERALL ATMOSPHERE:_____
_____

☐ BLACK-AND-WHITE   ☐ IN-COLOR   ☐ PREDOMINANT COLOR:_____

☐ IN THE DREAM   ☐ WATCHING THE DREAM HAPPEN   ☐ LUCID DREAM   ☐ RECURRING

ABOUT THE   ☐ PAST   ☐ PRESENT   ☐ FUTURE

HOW I FELT IN MY DREAM:_____
HOW I FEEL NOW: _____
LAST THING I ATE OR DRANK:_____
_____

LAST THING I REMEMBER BEFORE FALLING ASLEEP:_____
_____

MY
STRANGE
DREAM

DREAM TITLE _____ DATE: _____

_____

_____

_____

_____

_____

_____

_____

_____

_____

_____

_____

_____

_____

_____

VISUAL NOTES:

STRANGENESS METER

RIDICULOUSLY BORING	MEH	NORMAL	SAAAAY WHAT!?	HUMAN LANGUAGE CANNOT EXPLAIN THIS!

DREAM THEME

- ☐ ANIMALS
- ☐ FIRE
- ☐ LOSING TEETH
- ☐ SUPERNATURAL

- ☐ BEING CHASED
- ☐ FLYING
- ☐ MONEY
- ☐ TRAVEL

- ☐ BUGS
- ☐ FOOD / DRINK
- ☐ NAKED
- ☐ WATER

- ☐ CHILDHOOD
- ☐ HOME
- ☐ OUT-OF-BODY EXPERIENCE
- ☐ WEATHER

☐ OTHER:_____

MAIN CHARACTERS:_____

_____

LOCATION: _____

_____

OVERALL ATMOSPHERE: _____

_____

☐ BLACK-AND-WHITE ☐ IN-COLOR ☐ PREDOMINANT COLOR:_____

☐ IN THE DREAM ☐ WATCHING THE DREAM HAPPEN ☐ LUCID DREAM ☐ RECURRING

ABOUT THE ☐ PAST ☐ PRESENT ☐ FUTURE

HOW I FELT IN MY DREAM:_____

HOW I FEEL NOW: _____

LAST THING I ATE OR DRANK: _____

_____

LAST THING I REMEMBER BEFORE FALLING ASLEEP:_____

_____

MY
STRANGE
DREAM

DREAM TITLE _____ DATE: _____

_____
_____
_____
_____
_____
_____
_____
_____
_____
_____
_____
_____
_____
_____
_____
_____

VISUAL NOTES:

STRANGENESS METER

RIDICULOUSLY BORING — MEH — NORMAL — SAAAAY WHAT!? — HUMAN LANGUAGE CANNOT EXPLAIN THIS!

. . . .

DREAM THEME

☐ ANIMALS   ☐ BEING CHASED   ☐ BUGS   ☐ CHILDHOOD

☐ FIRE   ☐ FLYING   ☐ FOOD / DRINK   ☐ HOME

☐ LOSING TEETH   ☐ MONEY   ☐ NAKED   ☐ OUT-OF-BODY EXPERIENCE

☐ SUPERNATURAL   ☐ TRAVEL   ☐ WATER   ☐ WEATHER

☐ OTHER: _____

. . . .

MAIN CHARACTERS: _____

_____

LOCATION: _____

_____

OVERALL ATMOSPHERE: _____

_____

☐ BLACK-AND-WHITE   ☐ IN-COLOR   ☐ PREDOMINANT COLOR: _____

☐ IN THE DREAM   ☐ WATCHING THE DREAM HAPPEN   ☐ LUCID DREAM   ☐ RECURRING

ABOUT THE   ☐ PAST   ☐ PRESENT   ☐ FUTURE

HOW I FELT IN MY DREAM: _____

HOW I FEEL NOW: _____

LAST THING I ATE OR DRANK: _____

_____

LAST THING I REMEMBER BEFORE FALLING ASLEEP: _____

_____

MY
STRANGE
DREAM

DREAM TITLE _____ DATE: _____

_____
_____
_____
_____
_____
_____
_____
_____
_____
_____
_____
_____
_____
_____
_____

VISUAL NOTES:

STRANGENESS METER

|———————————|———————————|———————————|———————————|

RIDICULOUSLY   MEH   NORMAL   SAAAAY   HUMAN
BORING   WHAT!?   LANGUAGE
                                                       CANNOT
                                                     EXPLAIN THIS!

DREAM THEME

☐ ANIMALS   ☐ BEING CHASED   ☐ BUGS   ☐ CHILDHOOD

☐ FIRE   ☐ FLYING   ☐ FOOD / DRINK   ☐ HOME

☐ LOSING TEETH   ☐ MONEY   ☐ NAKED   ☐ OUT-OF-BODY EXPERIENCE

☐ SUPERNATURAL   ☐ TRAVEL   ☐ WATER   ☐ WEATHER

☐ OTHER: _____

MAIN CHARACTERS: _____
_____

LOCATION: _____
_____

OVERALL ATMOSPHERE: _____
_____

      ☐ BLACK-AND-WHITE   ☐ IN-COLOR   ☐ PREDOMINANT COLOR: _____

☐ IN THE DREAM   ☐ WATCHING THE DREAM HAPPEN   ☐ LUCID DREAM   ☐ RECURRING
               ABOUT THE   ☐ PAST ☐ PRESENT ☐ FUTURE

HOW I FELT IN MY DREAM: _____
HOW I FEEL NOW: _____

LAST THING I ATE OR DRANK: _____
_____

LAST THING I REMEMBER BEFORE FALLING ASLEEP: _____
_____

MY
STRANGE
DREAM

DREAM TITLE _____ DATE: _____

_____
_____
_____
_____
_____
_____
_____
_____
_____
_____
_____
_____
_____
_____
_____

VISUAL NOTES:

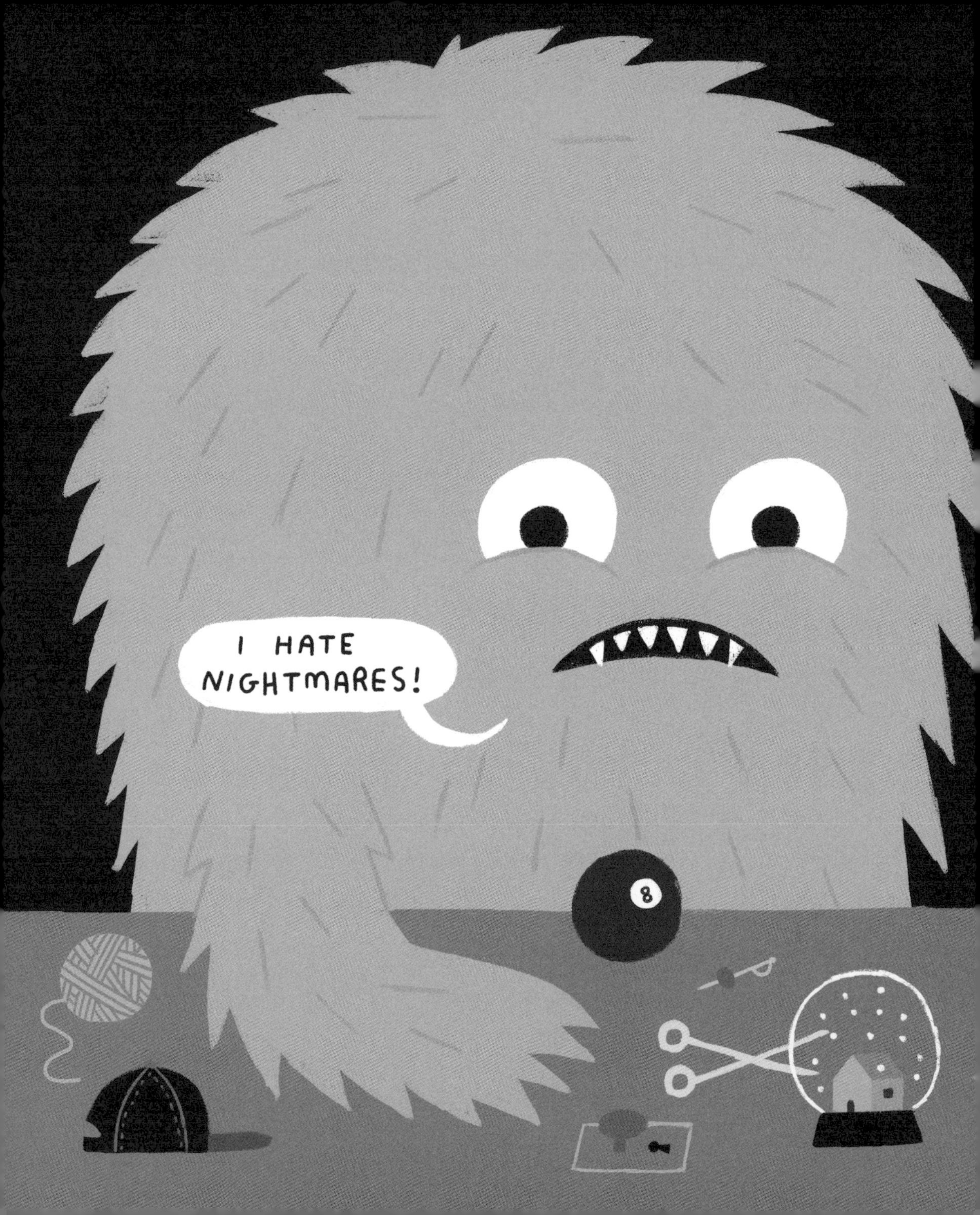
I HATE NIGHTMARES!

STRANGENESS METER

RIDICULOUSLY BORING	MEH	NORMAL	SAAAAY WHAT!?	HUMAN LANGUAGE CANNOT EXPLAIN THIS!

DREAM THEME

☐ ANIMALS   ☐ BEING CHASED   ☐ BUGS   ☐ CHILDHOOD

☐ FIRE   ☐ FLYING   ☐ FOOD / DRINK   ☐ HOME

☐ LOSING TEETH   ☐ MONEY   ☐ NAKED   ☐ OUT-OF-BODY EXPERIENCE

☐ SUPERNATURAL   ☐ TRAVEL   ☐ WATER   ☐ WEATHER

☐ OTHER: _____

MAIN CHARACTERS: _____

_____

LOCATION: _____

_____

OVERALL ATMOSPHERE: _____

_____

☐ BLACK-AND-WHITE   ☐ IN-COLOR   ☐ PREDOMINANT COLOR: _____

☐ IN THE DREAM   ☐ WATCHING THE DREAM HAPPEN   ☐ LUCID DREAM   ☐ RECURRING

ABOUT THE   ☐ PAST   ☐ PRESENT   ☐ FUTURE

HOW I FELT IN MY DREAM: _____

HOW I FEEL NOW: _____

LAST THING I ATE OR DRANK: _____

LAST THING I REMEMBER BEFORE FALLING ASLEEP: _____

_____

MY
STRANGE
DREAM

DREAM TITLE _____ DATE: _____

_____
_____
_____
_____
_____
_____
_____
_____
_____
_____
_____
_____
_____
_____
_____
_____

VISUAL NOTES:

STRANGENESS METER

RIDICULOUSLY BORING	MEH	NORMAL	SAAAAY WHAT!?	HUMAN LANGUAGE CANNOT EXPLAIN THIS!

DREAM THEME

☐ ANIMALS   ☐ BEING CHASED   ☐ BUGS   ☐ CHILDHOOD

☐ FIRE   ☐ FLYING   ☐ FOOD / DRINK   ☐ HOME

☐ LOSING TEETH   ☐ MONEY   ☐ NAKED   ☐ OUT-OF-BODY EXPERIENCE

☐ SUPERNATURAL   ☐ TRAVEL   ☐ WATER   ☐ WEATHER

☐ OTHER: _____

MAIN CHARACTERS: _____

_____

LOCATION: _____

_____

OVERALL ATMOSPHERE: _____

_____

☐ BLACK-AND-WHITE   ☐ IN-COLOR   ☐ PREDOMINANT COLOR: _____

☐ IN THE DREAM   ☐ WATCHING THE DREAM HAPPEN   ☐ LUCID DREAM   ☐ RECURRING

ABOUT THE   ☐ PAST   ☐ PRESENT   ☐ FUTURE

HOW I FELT IN MY DREAM: _____

HOW I FEEL NOW: _____

LAST THING I ATE OR DRANK: _____

_____

LAST THING I REMEMBER BEFORE FALLING ASLEEP: _____

_____

MY
STRANGE
DREAM

DREAM TITLE _____ DATE: _____

_____
_____
_____
_____
_____
_____
_____
_____
_____
_____
_____
_____
_____
_____
_____
_____

VISUAL NOTES:

STRANGENESS METER

RIDICULOUSLY BORING — MEH — NORMAL — SAAAAY WHAT!? — HUMAN LANGUAGE CANNOT EXPLAIN THIS!

DREAM THEME

☐ ANIMALS   ☐ BEING CHASED   ☐ BUGS   ☐ CHILDHOOD

☐ FIRE   ☐ FLYING   ☐ FOOD / DRINK   ☐ HOME

☐ LOSING TEETH   ☐ MONEY   ☐ NAKED   ☐ OUT-OF-BODY EXPERIENCE

☐ SUPERNATURAL   ☐ TRAVEL   ☐ WATER   ☐ WEATHER

☐ OTHER:_____

MAIN CHARACTERS:_____

LOCATION:_____

OVERALL ATMOSPHERE:_____

☐ BLACK-AND-WHITE ☐ IN-COLOR ☐ PREDOMINANT COLOR:_____

☐ IN THE DREAM ☐ WATCHING THE DREAM HAPPEN ☐ LUCID DREAM ☐ RECURRING

ABOUT THE ☐ PAST ☐ PRESENT ☐ FUTURE

HOW I FELT IN MY DREAM:_____

HOW I FEEL NOW:_____

LAST THING I ATE OR DRANK:_____

LAST THING I REMEMBER BEFORE FALLING ASLEEP:_____

MY
STRANGE
DREAM

DREAM TITLE _____ DATE: _____

_____
_____
_____
_____
_____
_____
_____
_____
_____
_____
_____
_____
_____
_____
_____
_____
_____

VISUAL NOTES:

STRANGENESS METER

RIDICULOUSLY BORING	MEH	NORMAL	SAAAAY WHAT!?	HUMAN LANGUAGE CANNOT EXPLAIN THIS!

DREAM THEME

☐ ANIMALS   ☐ BEING CHASED   ☐ BUGS   ☐ CHILDHOOD
☐ FIRE   ☐ FLYING   ☐ FOOD / DRINK   ☐ HOME
☐ LOSING TEETH   ☐ MONEY   ☐ NAKED   ☐ OUT-OF-BODY EXPERIENCE
☐ SUPERNATURAL   ☐ TRAVEL   ☐ WATER   ☐ WEATHER

☐ OTHER: _____

MAIN CHARACTERS: _____
_____

LOCATION: _____
_____

OVERALL ATMOSPHERE: _____
_____

☐ BLACK-AND-WHITE ☐ IN-COLOR ☐ PREDOMINANT COLOR: _____

☐ IN THE DREAM ☐ WATCHING THE DREAM HAPPEN ☐ LUCID DREAM ☐ RECURRING
ABOUT THE ☐ PAST ☐ PRESENT ☐ FUTURE

HOW I FELT IN MY DREAM: _____
HOW I FEEL NOW: _____
LAST THING I ATE OR DRANK: _____
_____
LAST THING I REMEMBER BEFORE FALLING ASLEEP: _____
_____

MY
STRANGE
DREAM

DREAM TITLE _____ DATE: _____

_____
_____
_____
_____
_____
_____
_____
_____
_____
_____
_____
_____
_____
_____
_____
_____

VISUAL NOTES:

STRANGENESS METER

RIDICULOUSLY BORING — MEH — NORMAL — SAAAAY WHAT!? — HUMAN LANGUAGE CANNOT EXPLAIN THIS!

DREAM THEME

☐ ANIMALS   ☐ BEING CHASED   ☐ BUGS   ☐ CHILDHOOD
☐ FIRE   ☐ FLYING   ☐ FOOD / DRINK ☐ HOME
☐ LOSING TEETH   ☐ MONEY   ☐ NAKED   ☐ OUT-OF-BODY EXPERIENCE
☐ SUPERNATURAL   ☐ TRAVEL   ☐ WATER   ☐ WEATHER

☐ OTHER: _____

MAIN CHARACTERS: _____
_____

LOCATION: _____
_____

OVERALL ATMOSPHERE: _____
_____

☐ BLACK-AND-WHITE ☐ IN-COLOR ☐ PREDOMINANT COLOR: _____

☐ IN THE DREAM ☐ WATCHING THE DREAM HAPPEN ☐ LUCID DREAM ☐ RECURRING
ABOUT THE ☐ PAST ☐ PRESENT ☐ FUTURE

HOW I FELT IN MY DREAM: _____
HOW I FEEL NOW: _____
LAST THING I ATE OR DRANK: _____

LAST THING I REMEMBER BEFORE FALLING ASLEEP: _____
_____

MY
STRANGE
DREAM

DREAM TITLE _____ DATE: _____

_____
_____
_____
_____
_____
_____
_____
_____
_____
_____
_____
_____
_____
_____
_____

VISUAL NOTES:

STRANGENESS METER

RIDICULOUSLY BORING	MEH	NORMAL	SAAAAY WHAT!?	HUMAN LANGUAGE CANNOT EXPLAIN THIS!

DREAM THEME

☐ ANIMALS   ☐ BEING CHASED   ☐ BUGS   ☐ CHILDHOOD

☐ FIRE   ☐ FLYING   ☐ FOOD / DRINK   ☐ HOME

☐ LOSING TEETH   ☐ MONEY   ☐ NAKED   ☐ OUT-OF-BODY EXPERIENCE

☐ SUPERNATURAL   ☐ TRAVEL   ☐ WATER   ☐ WEATHER

☐ OTHER: _____

MAIN CHARACTERS: _____
_____

LOCATION: _____
_____

OVERALL ATMOSPHERE: _____
_____

☐ BLACK-AND-WHITE   ☐ IN-COLOR   ☐ PREDOMINANT COLOR: _____

☐ IN THE DREAM   ☐ WATCHING THE DREAM HAPPEN   ☐ LUCID DREAM   ☐ RECURRING

ABOUT THE   ☐ PAST   ☐ PRESENT   ☐ FUTURE

HOW I FELT IN MY DREAM: _____
HOW I FEEL NOW: _____
LAST THING I ATE OR DRANK: _____

LAST THING I REMEMBER BEFORE FALLING ASLEEP: _____
_____

MY STRANGE DREAM

DREAM TITLE _____ DATE: _____

_____
_____
_____
_____
_____
_____
_____
_____
_____
_____
_____
_____
_____
_____

VISUAL NOTES:

STRANGENESS METER

RIDICULOUSLY BORING | MEH | NORMAL | SAAAAY WHAT!? | HUMAN LANGUAGE CANNOT EXPLAIN THIS!

DREAM THEME

☐ ANIMALS   ☐ BEING CHASED   ☐ BUGS   ☐ CHILDHOOD
☐ FIRE   ☐ FLYING   ☐ FOOD / DRINK ☐ HOME
☐ LOSING TEETH ☐ MONEY   ☐ NAKED   ☐ OUT-OF-BODY EXPERIENCE
☐ SUPERNATURAL ☐ TRAVEL   ☐ WATER   ☐ WEATHER

☐ OTHER: _____

MAIN CHARACTERS: _____

LOCATION: _____

OVERALL ATMOSPHERE: _____

☐ BLACK-AND-WHITE ☐ IN-COLOR ☐ PREDOMINANT COLOR: _____

☐ IN THE DREAM ☐ WATCHING THE DREAM HAPPEN ☐ LUCID DREAM ☐ RECURRING
ABOUT THE ☐ PAST ☐ PRESENT ☐ FUTURE

HOW I FELT IN MY DREAM: _____
HOW I FEEL NOW: _____
LAST THING I ATE OR DRANK: _____

LAST THING I REMEMBER BEFORE FALLING ASLEEP: _____

MY
STRANGE
DREAM

DREAM TITLE _____ DATE: _____

_____
_____
_____
_____
_____
_____
_____
_____
_____
_____
_____
_____
_____
_____

VISUAL NOTES:

STRANGENESS METER

|————————|————————|————————|————————|
RIDICULOUSLY   MEH   NORMAL   SAAAAY   HUMAN
BORING   WHAT!?   LANGUAGE
                                                                 CANNOT
                                                                 EXPLAIN THIS!

DREAM THEME

☐ ANIMALS   ☐ BEING CHASED   ☐ BUGS   ☐ CHILDHOOD
☐ FIRE   ☐ FLYING   ☐ FOOD / DRINK   ☐ HOME
☐ LOSING TEETH   ☐ MONEY   ☐ NAKED   ☐ OUT-OF-BODY EXPERIENCE
☐ SUPERNATURAL   ☐ TRAVEL   ☐ WATER   ☐ WEATHER

☐ OTHER:_____

MAIN CHARACTERS:_____
_____

LOCATION: _____
_____

OVERALL ATMOSPHERE:_____
_____

☐ BLACK-AND-WHITE ☐ IN-COLOR ☐ PREDOMINANT COLOR:_____

☐ IN THE DREAM ☐ WATCHING THE DREAM HAPPEN ☐ LUCID DREAM ☐ RECURRING
ABOUT THE ☐ PAST ☐ PRESENT ☐ FUTURE

HOW I FELT IN MY DREAM:_____
HOW I FEEL NOW:_____
LAST THING I ATE OR DRANK:_____
_____

LAST THING I REMEMBER BEFORE FALLING ASLEEP:_____
_____

MY
STRANGE
DREAM

DREAM TITLE _____ DATE: _____

_____
_____
_____
_____
_____
_____
_____
_____
_____
_____
_____
_____
_____
_____
_____
_____

VISUAL NOTES:

STRANGENESS METER

RIDICULOUSLY BORING	MEH	NORMAL	SAAAAY WHAT!?	HUMAN LANGUAGE CANNOT EXPLAIN THIS!

. . . .

DREAM THEME

☐ ANIMALS   ☐ BEING CHASED   ☐ BUGS   ☐ CHILDHOOD

☐ FIRE   ☐ FLYING   ☐ FOOD / DRINK   ☐ HOME

☐ LOSING TEETH   ☐ MONEY   ☐ NAKED   ☐ OUT-OF-BODY EXPERIENCE

☐ SUPERNATURAL   ☐ TRAVEL   ☐ WATER   ☐ WEATHER

☐ OTHER:_____

. . . .

MAIN CHARACTERS:_____
_____

LOCATION: _____
_____

OVERALL ATMOSPHERE: _____
_____

☐ BLACK-AND-WHITE   ☐ IN-COLOR ☐ PREDOMINANT COLOR:_____

☐ IN THE DREAM   ☐ WATCHING THE DREAM HAPPEN   ☐ LUCID DREAM ☐ RECURRING

ABOUT THE   ☐ PAST ☐ PRESENT ☐ FUTURE

HOW I FELT IN MY DREAM:_____

HOW I FEEL NOW:_____

LAST THING I ATE OR DRANK: _____
_____

LAST THING I REMEMBER BEFORE FALLING ASLEEP:_____
_____

MY
STRANGE
DREAM

DREAM TITLE _____ DATE: _____

VISUAL NOTES:

STRANGENESS METER

RIDICULOUSLY BORING — MEH — NORMAL — SAAAAY WHAT!? — HUMAN LANGUAGE CANNOT EXPLAIN THIS!

DREAM THEME

☐ ANIMALS   ☐ BEING CHASED   ☐ BUGS   ☐ CHILDHOOD

☐ FIRE   ☐ FLYING   ☐ FOOD / DRINK   ☐ HOME

☐ LOSING TEETH   ☐ MONEY   ☐ NAKED   ☐ OUT-OF-BODY EXPERIENCE

☐ SUPERNATURAL   ☐ TRAVEL   ☐ WATER   ☐ WEATHER

☐ OTHER: _____

MAIN CHARACTERS: _____

_____

LOCATION: _____

_____

OVERALL ATMOSPHERE: _____

_____

☐ BLACK-AND-WHITE   ☐ IN-COLOR   ☐ PREDOMINANT COLOR: _____

☐ IN THE DREAM   ☐ WATCHING THE DREAM HAPPEN   ☐ LUCID DREAM   ☐ RECURRING

ABOUT THE   ☐ PAST   ☐ PRESENT   ☐ FUTURE

HOW I FELT IN MY DREAM: _____

HOW I FEEL NOW: _____

LAST THING I ATE OR DRANK: _____

_____

LAST THING I REMEMBER BEFORE FALLING ASLEEP: _____

_____

MY
STRANGE
DREAM

DREAM TITLE _____ DATE: _____

_____
_____
_____
_____
_____
_____
_____
_____
_____
_____
_____
_____
_____
_____
_____
_____
_____

VISUAL NOTES:

STRANGENESS METER

RIDICULOUSLY BORING	MEH	NORMAL	SAAAAY WHAT!?	HUMAN LANGUAGE CANNOT EXPLAIN THIS!

DREAM THEME

☐ ANIMALS   ☐ BEING CHASED   ☐ BUGS   ☐ CHILDHOOD

☐ FIRE   ☐ FLYING   ☐ FOOD / DRINK   ☐ HOME

☐ LOSING TEETH   ☐ MONEY   ☐ NAKED   ☐ OUT-OF-BODY EXPERIENCE

☐ SUPERNATURAL   ☐ TRAVEL   ☐ WATER   ☐ WEATHER

☐ OTHER:_____

MAIN CHARACTERS:_____
_____

LOCATION: _____
_____

OVERALL ATMOSPHERE:_____
_____

☐ BLACK-AND-WHITE   ☐ IN-COLOR   ☐ PREDOMINANT COLOR:_____

☐ IN THE DREAM   ☐ WATCHING THE DREAM HAPPEN   ☐ LUCID DREAM   ☐ RECURRING

ABOUT THE   ☐ PAST   ☐ PRESENT   ☐ FUTURE

HOW I FELT IN MY DREAM:_____
HOW I FEEL NOW: _____
LAST THING I ATE OR DRANK: _____
_____

LAST THING I REMEMBER BEFORE FALLING ASLEEP:_____
_____

MY STRANGE DREAM

DREAM TITLE _____ DATE: _____

_____
_____
_____
_____
_____
_____
_____
_____
_____
_____
_____
_____
_____
_____
_____

VISUAL NOTES:

STRANGENESS METER

RIDICULOUSLY BORING	MEH	NORMAL	SAAAAY WHAT!?	HUMAN LANGUAGE CANNOT EXPLAIN THIS!

- -

DREAM THEME

☐ ANIMALS   ☐ BEING CHASED   ☐ BUGS   ☐ CHILDHOOD

☐ FIRE   ☐ FLYING   ☐ FOOD / DRINK   ☐ HOME

☐ LOSING TEETH   ☐ MONEY   ☐ NAKED   ☐ OUT-OF-BODY EXPERIENCE

☐ SUPERNATURAL   ☐ TRAVEL   ☐ WATER   ☐ WEATHER

☐ OTHER:_____

- -

MAIN CHARACTERS:_____

_____

LOCATION: _____

_____

OVERALL ATMOSPHERE:_____

_____

     ☐ BLACK-AND-WHITE   ☐ IN-COLOR   ☐ PREDOMINANT COLOR:_____

☐ IN THE DREAM   ☐ WATCHING THE DREAM HAPPEN   ☐ LUCID DREAM   ☐ RECURRING

         ABOUT THE   ☐ PAST   ☐ PRESENT   ☐ FUTURE

HOW I FELT IN MY DREAM:_____

HOW I FEEL NOW:_____

LAST THING I ATE OR DRANK:_____

_____

LAST THING I REMEMBER BEFORE FALLING ASLEEP:_____

_____

MY
STRANGE
DREAM

DREAM TITLE _____ DATE: _____

_____
_____
_____
_____
_____
_____
_____
_____
_____
_____
_____
_____
_____
_____
_____
_____

VISUAL NOTES:

STRANGENESS METER

RIDICULOUSLY BORING	MEH	NORMAL	SAAAAY WHAT!?	HUMAN LANGUAGE CANNOT EXPLAIN THIS!

DREAM THEME

- ☐ ANIMALS
- ☐ FIRE
- ☐ LOSING TEETH
- ☐ SUPERNATURAL

- ☐ BEING CHASED
- ☐ FLYING
- ☐ MONEY
- ☐ TRAVEL

- ☐ BUGS
- ☐ FOOD / DRINK
- ☐ NAKED
- ☐ WATER

- ☐ CHILDHOOD
- ☐ HOME
- ☐ OUT-OF-BODY EXPERIENCE
- ☐ WEATHER

☐ OTHER:_____

MAIN CHARACTERS:_____
_____

LOCATION: _____
_____

OVERALL ATMOSPHERE:_____
_____

☐ BLACK-AND-WHITE   ☐ IN-COLOR   ☐ PREDOMINANT COLOR:_____

☐ IN THE DREAM   ☐ WATCHING THE DREAM HAPPEN   ☐ LUCID DREAM   ☐ RECURRING

ABOUT THE   ☐ PAST   ☐ PRESENT   ☐ FUTURE

HOW I FELT IN MY DREAM:_____
HOW I FEEL NOW:_____
LAST THING I ATE OR DRANK: _____
_____
LAST THING I REMEMBER BEFORE FALLING ASLEEP:_____
_____

MY STRANGE DREAM

DREAM TITLE _____ DATE: _____

_____
_____
_____
_____
_____
_____
_____
_____
_____
_____
_____
_____
_____
_____
_____
_____

VISUAL NOTES:

STRANGENESS METER

|————————|————————|————————|————————|
RIDICULOUSLY   MEH   NORMAL   SAAAAY   HUMAN
BORING   WHAT!?   LANGUAGE
                                                            CANNOT
                                                            EXPLAIN THIS!

· ·

DREAM THEME

☐ ANIMALS   ☐ BEING CHASED   ☐ BUGS   ☐ CHILDHOOD

☐ FIRE   ☐ FLYING   ☐ FOOD / DRINK   ☐ HOME

☐ LOSING TEETH   ☐ MONEY   ☐ NAKED   ☐ OUT-OF-BODY EXPERIENCE

☐ SUPERNATURAL   ☐ TRAVEL   ☐ WATER   ☐ WEATHER

☐ OTHER:_____

· ·

MAIN CHARACTERS:_____

LOCATION:_____

OVERALL ATMOSPHERE:_____

☐ BLACK-AND-WHITE   ☐ IN-COLOR   ☐ PREDOMINANT COLOR:_____

☐ IN THE DREAM   ☐ WATCHING THE DREAM HAPPEN   ☐ LUCID DREAM   ☐ RECURRING

        ABOUT THE   ☐ PAST   ☐ PRESENT   ☐ FUTURE

HOW I FELT IN MY DREAM:_____

HOW I FEEL NOW:_____

LAST THING I ATE OR DRANK:_____

LAST THING I REMEMBER BEFORE FALLING ASLEEP:_____

MY
STRANGE
DREAM

DREAM TITLE _____ DATE: _____

_____
_____
_____
_____
_____
_____
_____
_____
_____
_____
_____
_____
_____
_____
_____

VISUAL NOTES:

ISN'T IT STRANGE THAT ANIMALS DREAM?
I DIDN'T KNOW THEY DID.
WELL, MAMMALS DO, ANYWAY.

STRANGENESS METER

RIDICULOUSLY BORING   MEH   NORMAL   SAAAAY WHAT!?   HUMAN LANGUAGE CANNOT EXPLAIN THIS!

DREAM THEME

□ ANIMALS   □ BEING CHASED   □ BUGS   □ CHILDHOOD

□ FIRE   □ FLYING   □ FOOD / DRINK   □ HOME

□ LOSING TEETH   □ MONEY   □ NAKED   □ OUT-OF-BODY EXPERIENCE

□ SUPERNATURAL   □ TRAVEL   □ WATER   □ WEATHER

□ OTHER: _____

MAIN CHARACTERS: _____

_____

LOCATION: _____

_____

OVERALL ATMOSPHERE: _____

_____

□ BLACK-AND-WHITE   □ IN-COLOR   □ PREDOMINANT COLOR: _____

□ IN THE DREAM   □ WATCHING THE DREAM HAPPEN   □ LUCID DREAM   □ RECURRING

ABOUT THE   □ PAST   □ PRESENT   □ FUTURE

HOW I FELT IN MY DREAM: _____

HOW I FEEL NOW: _____

LAST THING I ATE OR DRANK: _____

LAST THING I REMEMBER BEFORE FALLING ASLEEP: _____

_____

MY
STRANGE
DREAM

DREAM TITLE _____ DATE: _____

_____
_____
_____
_____
_____
_____
_____
_____
_____
_____
_____
_____
_____
_____
_____
_____
_____
_____

VISUAL NOTES:

STRANGENESS METER

RIDICULOUSLY BORING — MEH — NORMAL — SAAAAY WHAT!? — HUMAN LANGUAGE CANNOT EXPLAIN THIS!

DREAM THEME

☐ ANIMALS   ☐ BEING CHASED   ☐ BUGS   ☐ CHILDHOOD
☐ FIRE   ☐ FLYING   ☐ FOOD / DRINK   ☐ HOME
☐ LOSING TEETH   ☐ MONEY   ☐ NAKED   ☐ OUT-OF-BODY EXPERIENCE
☐ SUPERNATURAL   ☐ TRAVEL   ☐ WATER   ☐ WEATHER

☐ OTHER: _____

MAIN CHARACTERS: _____

LOCATION: _____

OVERALL ATMOSPHERE: _____

☐ BLACK-AND-WHITE   ☐ IN-COLOR   ☐ PREDOMINANT COLOR: _____

☐ IN THE DREAM   ☐ WATCHING THE DREAM HAPPEN   ☐ LUCID DREAM   ☐ RECURRING
ABOUT THE   ☐ PAST ☐ PRESENT ☐ FUTURE

HOW I FELT IN MY DREAM: _____
HOW I FEEL NOW: _____
LAST THING I ATE OR DRANK: _____

LAST THING I REMEMBER BEFORE FALLING ASLEEP: _____

MY STRANGE DREAM

DREAM TITLE _____ DATE: _____

_____
_____
_____
_____
_____
_____
_____
_____
_____
_____
_____
_____
_____
_____
_____
_____

VISUAL NOTES:

STRANGENESS METER

RIDICULOUSLY BORING — MEH — NORMAL — SAAAAY WHAT!? — HUMAN LANGUAGE CANNOT EXPLAIN THIS!

DREAM THEME

- ☐ ANIMALS
- ☐ FIRE
- ☐ LOSING TEETH
- ☐ SUPERNATURAL

- ☐ BEING CHASED
- ☐ FLYING
- ☐ MONEY
- ☐ TRAVEL

- ☐ BUGS
- ☐ FOOD / DRINK
- ☐ NAKED
- ☐ WATER

- ☐ CHILDHOOD
- ☐ HOME
- ☐ OUT-OF-BODY EXPERIENCE
- ☐ WEATHER

☐ OTHER: _____

MAIN CHARACTERS: _____

LOCATION: _____

OVERALL ATMOSPHERE: _____

☐ BLACK-AND-WHITE ☐ IN-COLOR ☐ PREDOMINANT COLOR: _____

☐ IN THE DREAM ☐ WATCHING THE DREAM HAPPEN ☐ LUCID DREAM ☐ RECURRING

ABOUT THE ☐ PAST ☐ PRESENT ☐ FUTURE

HOW I FELT IN MY DREAM: _____
HOW I FEEL NOW: _____
LAST THING I ATE OR DRANK: _____

LAST THING I REMEMBER BEFORE FALLING ASLEEP: _____

MY
STRANGE
DREAM

DREAM TITLE _____ DATE: _____

_____
_____
_____
_____
_____
_____
_____
_____
_____
_____
_____
_____
_____
_____
_____

VISUAL NOTES:

STRANGENESS METER

RIDICULOUSLY BORING	MEH	NORMAL	SAAAAY WHAT!?	HUMAN LANGUAGE CANNOT EXPLAIN THIS!

· ·

DREAM THEME

☐ ANIMALS ☐ BEING CHASED ☐ BUGS ☐ CHILDHOOD

☐ FIRE ☐ FLYING ☐ FOOD / DRINK ☐ HOME

☐ LOSING TEETH ☐ MONEY ☐ NAKED ☐ OUT-OF-BODY EXPERIENCE

☐ SUPERNATURAL ☐ TRAVEL ☐ WATER ☐ WEATHER

☐ OTHER: _____

· ·

MAIN CHARACTERS: _____
_____

LOCATION: _____
_____

OVERALL ATMOSPHERE: _____
_____

☐ BLACK-AND-WHITE ☐ IN-COLOR ☐ PREDOMINANT COLOR: _____

☐ IN THE DREAM ☐ WATCHING THE DREAM HAPPEN ☐ LUCID DREAM ☐ RECURRING

ABOUT THE ☐ PAST ☐ PRESENT ☐ FUTURE

HOW I FELT IN MY DREAM: _____
HOW I FEEL NOW: _____
LAST THING I ATE OR DRANK: _____

LAST THING I REMEMBER BEFORE FALLING ASLEEP: _____
_____

MY
STRANGE
DREAM

DREAM TITLE _____ DATE: _____

_____
_____
_____
_____
_____
_____
_____
_____
_____
_____
_____
_____
_____
_____
_____
_____

VISUAL NOTES:

STRANGENESS METER

RIDICULOUSLY BORING   MEH   NORMAL   SAAAAY WHAT!?   HUMAN LANGUAGE CAN NOT EXPLAIN THIS!

DREAM THEME

- ☐ ANIMALS
- ☐ FIRE
- ☐ LOSING TEETH
- ☐ SUPERNATURAL

- ☐ BEING CHASED
- ☐ FLYING
- ☐ MONEY
- ☐ TRAVEL

- ☐ BUGS
- ☐ FOOD / DRINK
- ☐ NAKED
- ☐ WATER

- ☐ CHILDHOOD
- ☐ HOME
- ☐ OUT-OF-BODY EXPERIENCE
- ☐ WEATHER

☐ OTHER:_____

MAIN CHARACTERS:_____
_____

LOCATION: _____
_____

OVERALL ATMOSPHERE: _____
_____

☐ BLACK-AND-WHITE ☐ IN-COLOR ☐ PREDOMINANT COLOR:_____

☐ IN THE DREAM ☐ WATCHING THE DREAM HAPPEN ☐ LUCID DREAM ☐ RECURRING

ABOUT THE ☐ PAST ☐ PRESENT ☐ FUTURE

HOW I FELT IN MY DREAM:_____
HOW I FEEL NOW: _____
LAST THING I ATE OR DRANK:_____
_____

LAST THING I REMEMBER BEFORE FALLING ASLEEP:_____
_____

MY
STRANGE
DREAM

DREAM TITLE _____ DATE: _____

_____
_____
_____
_____
_____
_____
_____
_____
_____
_____
_____
_____
_____
_____
_____

VISUAL NOTES:

STRANGENESS METER

RIDICULOUSLY BORING	MEH	NORMAL	SAAAAY WHAT!?	HUMAN LANGUAGE CAN NOT EXPLAIN THIS!

. . . .

DREAM THEME

☐ ANIMALS   ☐ BEING CHASED   ☐ BUGS   ☐ CHILDHOOD

☐ FIRE   ☐ FLYING   ☐ FOOD / DRINK   ☐ HOME

☐ LOSING TEETH   ☐ MONEY   ☐ NAKED   ☐ OUT-OF-BODY EXPERIENCE

☐ SUPERNATURAL   ☐ TRAVEL   ☐ WATER   ☐ WEATHER

☐ OTHER:_____

. . . .

MAIN CHARACTERS:_____

_____

LOCATION:_____

_____

OVERALL ATMOSPHERE:_____

_____

☐ BLACK-AND-WHITE   ☐ IN-COLOR   ☐ PREDOMINANT COLOR:_____

☐ IN THE DREAM   ☐ WATCHING THE DREAM HAPPEN   ☐ LUCID DREAM   ☐ RECURRING

ABOUT THE   ☐ PAST   ☐ PRESENT   ☐ FUTURE

HOW I FELT IN MY DREAM:_____

HOW I FEEL NOW:_____

LAST THING I ATE OR DRANK:_____

LAST THING I REMEMBER BEFORE FALLING ASLEEP:_____

_____

MY
STRANGE
DREAM

DREAM TITLE _____ DATE: _____

_____
_____
_____
_____
_____
_____
_____
_____
_____
_____
_____
_____
_____
_____
_____
_____
_____

VISUAL NOTES:

STRANGENESS METER

RIDICULOUSLY BORING   MEH   NORMAL   SAAAAY WHAT!?   HUMAN LANGUAGE CANNOT EXPLAIN THIS!

. . . .

DREAM THEME

☐ ANIMALS   ☐ BEING CHASED   ☐ BUGS   ☐ CHILDHOOD

☐ FIRE   ☐ FLYING   ☐ FOOD / DRINK   ☐ HOME

☐ LOSING TEETH   ☐ MONEY   ☐ NAKED   ☐ OUT-OF-BODY EXPERIENCE

☐ SUPERNATURAL   ☐ TRAVEL   ☐ WATER   ☐ WEATHER

☐ OTHER: _____

. . . .

MAIN CHARACTERS: _____

_____

LOCATION: _____

_____

OVERALL ATMOSPHERE: _____

_____

☐ BLACK-AND-WHITE   ☐ IN-COLOR   ☐ PREDOMINANT COLOR: _____

☐ IN THE DREAM   ☐ WATCHING THE DREAM HAPPEN   ☐ LUCID DREAM   ☐ RECURRING

ABOUT THE   ☐ PAST   ☐ PRESENT   ☐ FUTURE

HOW I FELT IN MY DREAM: _____

HOW I FEEL NOW: _____

LAST THING I ATE OR DRANK: _____

_____

LAST THING I REMEMBER BEFORE FALLING ASLEEP: _____

_____

MY
STRANGE
DREAM

DREAM TITLE _____ DATE: _____

_____
_____
_____
_____
_____
_____
_____
_____
_____
_____
_____
_____
_____
_____
_____

VISUAL NOTES:

STRANGENESS METER

| RIDICULOUSLY BORING | MEH | NORMAL | SAAAAY WHAT!? | HUMAN LANGUAGE CANNOT EXPLAIN THIS! |

DREAM THEME

☐ ANIMALS   ☐ BEING CHASED   ☐ BUGS   ☐ CHILDHOOD
☐ FIRE   ☐ FLYING   ☐ FOOD / DRINK   ☐ HOME
☐ LOSING TEETH   ☐ MONEY   ☐ NAKED   ☐ OUT-OF-BODY EXPERIENCE
☐ SUPERNATURAL   ☐ TRAVEL   ☐ WATER   ☐ WEATHER

☐ OTHER: _____

MAIN CHARACTERS: _____
_____

LOCATION: _____
_____

OVERALL ATMOSPHERE: _____
_____

☐ BLACK-AND-WHITE   ☐ IN-COLOR   ☐ PREDOMINANT COLOR: _____
☐ IN THE DREAM   ☐ WATCHING THE DREAM HAPPEN   ☐ LUCID DREAM   ☐ RECURRING
ABOUT THE   ☐ PAST   ☐ PRESENT   ☐ FUTURE

HOW I FELT IN MY DREAM: _____
HOW I FEEL NOW: _____
LAST THING I ATE OR DRANK: _____
_____

LAST THING I REMEMBER BEFORE FALLING ASLEEP: _____
_____

MY STRANGE DREAM

DREAM TITLE _____ DATE: _____

_____
_____
_____
_____
_____
_____
_____
_____
_____
_____
_____
_____
_____
_____

VISUAL NOTES:

STRANGENESS METER

RIDICULOUSLY BORING	MEH	NORMAL	SAAAAY WHAT!?	HUMAN LANGUAGE CANNOT EXPLAIN THIS!

DREAM THEME

□ ANIMALS   □ BEING CHASED   □ BUGS   □ CHILDHOOD
□ FIRE   □ FLYING   □ FOOD / DRINK   □ HOME
□ LOSING TEETH   □ MONEY   □ NAKED   □ OUT-OF-BODY EXPERIENCE
□ SUPERNATURAL   □ TRAVEL   □ WATER   □ WEATHER

□ OTHER:_____

MAIN CHARACTERS:_____
_____

LOCATION: _____
_____

OVERALL ATMOSPHERE:_____
_____

　　　□ BLACK-AND-WHITE □ IN-COLOR □ PREDOMINANT COLOR:_____

□ IN THE DREAM □ WATCHING THE DREAM HAPPEN □ LUCID DREAM □ RECURRING
　　　　　　ABOUT THE □ PAST □ PRESENT □ FUTURE

HOW I FELT IN MY DREAM:_____
HOW I FEEL NOW: _____
LAST THING I ATE OR DRANK: _____
_____

LAST THING I REMEMBER BEFORE FALLING ASLEEP:_____
_____

MY
STRANGE
DREAM

DREAM TITLE _____ DATE: _____

_____
_____
_____
_____
_____
_____
_____
_____
_____
_____
_____
_____
_____
_____
_____
_____
_____

VISUAL NOTES:

STRANGENESS METER

RIDICULOUSLY BORING	MEH	NORMAL	SAAAAY WHAT!?	HUMAN LANGUAGE CANNOT EXPLAIN THIS!

DREAM THEME

☐ ANIMALS ☐ BEING CHASED ☐ BUGS ☐ CHILDHOOD

☐ FIRE ☐ FLYING ☐ FOOD / DRINK ☐ HOME

☐ LOSING TEETH ☐ MONEY ☐ NAKED ☐ OUT-OF-BODY EXPERIENCE

☐ SUPERNATURAL ☐ TRAVEL ☐ WATER ☐ WEATHER

☐ OTHER:_____

MAIN CHARACTERS:_____
_____

LOCATION: _____
_____

OVERALL ATMOSPHERE:_____
_____

☐ BLACK-AND-WHITE ☐ IN-COLOR ☐ PREDOMINANT COLOR:_____

☐ IN THE DREAM ☐ WATCHING THE DREAM HAPPEN ☐ LUCID DREAM ☐ RECURRING

ABOUT THE ☐ PAST ☐ PRESENT ☐ FUTURE

HOW I FELT IN MY DREAM:_____

HOW I FEEL NOW:_____

LAST THING I ATE OR DRANK:_____
_____

LAST THING I REMEMBER BEFORE FALLING ASLEEP:_____
_____

MY
STRANGE
DREAM

DREAM TITLE _____ DATE: _____

_____
_____
_____
_____
_____
_____
_____
_____
_____
_____
_____
_____
_____
_____
_____

VISUAL NOTES:

STRANGENESS METER

RIDICULOUSLY BORING   MEH   NORMAL   SAAAAY WHAT!?   HUMAN LANGUAGE CANNOT EXPLAIN THIS!

DREAM THEME

- ☐ ANIMALS
- ☐ FIRE
- ☐ LOSING TEETH
- ☐ SUPERNATURAL

- ☐ BEING CHASED
- ☐ FLYING
- ☐ MONEY
- ☐ TRAVEL

- ☐ BUGS
- ☐ FOOD / DRINK
- ☐ NAKED
- ☐ WATER

- ☐ CHILDHOOD
- ☐ HOME
- ☐ OUT-OF-BODY EXPERIENCE
- ☐ WEATHER

☐ OTHER: _____

MAIN CHARACTERS: _____
_____

LOCATION: _____
_____

OVERALL ATMOSPHERE: _____
_____

☐ BLACK-AND-WHITE   ☐ IN-COLOR   ☐ PREDOMINANT COLOR: _____

☐ IN THE DREAM   ☐ WATCHING THE DREAM HAPPEN   ☐ LUCID DREAM   ☐ RECURRING

ABOUT THE   ☐ PAST   ☐ PRESENT   ☐ FUTURE

HOW I FELT IN MY DREAM: _____

HOW I FEEL NOW: _____

LAST THING I ATE OR DRANK: _____
_____

LAST THING I REMEMBER BEFORE FALLING ASLEEP: _____
_____

DREAM TITLE _____ DATE

_____

_____

_____

_____

_____

_____

_____

_____

_____

_____

_____

_____

VISUAL NOTES:

STRANGENESS METER

RIDICULOUSLY BORING — MEH — NORMAL — SAAAAY WHAT!? — HUMAN LANGUAGE CANNOT EXPLAIN THIS!

. . . .

DREAM THEME

☐ ANIMALS   ☐ BEING CHASED   ☐ BUGS   ☐ CHILDHOOD
☐ FIRE   ☐ FLYING   ☐ FOOD / DRINK   ☐ HOME
☐ LOSING TEETH   ☐ MONEY   ☐ NAKED   ☐ OUT-OF-BODY EXPERIENCE
☐ SUPERNATURAL   ☐ TRAVEL   ☐ WATER   ☐ WEATHER

☐ OTHER: _____

. . . .

MAIN CHARACTERS: _____
_____

LOCATION: _____
_____

OVERALL ATMOSPHERE: _____
_____

☐ BLACK-AND-WHITE ☐ IN-COLOR ☐ PREDOMINANT COLOR: _____

☐ IN THE DREAM ☐ WATCHING THE DREAM HAPPEN ☐ LUCID DREAM ☐ RECURRING
ABOUT THE ☐ PAST ☐ PRESENT ☐ FUTURE

HOW I FELT IN MY DREAM: _____
HOW I FEEL NOW: _____
LAST THING I ATE OR DRANK: _____
_____

LAST THING I REMEMBER BEFORE FALLING ASLEEP: _____
_____

MY STRANGE DREAM

DREAM TITLE _____ DATE: _____

_____
_____
_____
_____
_____
_____
_____
_____
_____
_____
_____
_____
_____
_____
_____

VISUAL NOTES:

STRANGENESS METER

RIDICULOUSLY BORING	MEH	NORMAL	SAAAAY WHAT!?	HUMAN LANGUAGE CANNOT EXPLAIN THIS!

DREAM THEME

☐ ANIMALS ☐ BEING CHASED ☐ BUGS ☐ CHILDHOOD

☐ FIRE ☐ FLYING ☐ FOOD / DRINK ☐ HOME

☐ LOSING TEETH ☐ MONEY ☐ NAKED ☐ OUT-OF-BODY EXPERIENCE

☐ SUPERNATURAL ☐ TRAVEL ☐ WATER ☐ WEATHER

☐ OTHER: _____

MAIN CHARACTERS: _____
_____

LOCATION: _____
_____

OVERALL ATMOSPHERE: _____
_____

☐ BLACK-AND-WHITE ☐ IN-COLOR ☐ PREDOMINANT COLOR: _____

☐ IN THE DREAM ☐ WATCHING THE DREAM HAPPEN ☐ LUCID DREAM ☐ RECURRING

ABOUT THE ☐ PAST ☐ PRESENT ☐ FUTURE

HOW I FELT IN MY DREAM: _____

HOW I FEEL NOW: _____

LAST THING I ATE OR DRANK: _____
_____

LAST THING I REMEMBER BEFORE FALLING ASLEEP: _____
_____

MY
STRANGE
DREAM

DREAM TITLE _____ DATE: _____

_____
_____
_____
_____
_____
_____
_____
_____
_____
_____
_____
_____
_____
_____
_____

VISUAL NOTES: